Tell Them I'm Real

Tell Them I'm Real

Real life miracles of God's love
from England to Chile and back

Arnold V Page

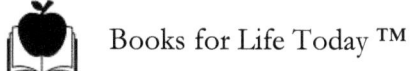 Books for Life Today ™

Tell Them I'm Real by Arnold V Page is an inspiring account of a life shaped by faith, miracles, and an unwavering belief in God's love. Spanning decades, the book recounts the author's journey from his early struggles with faith to his transformative experiences as a minister and missionary. His humility and vulnerability remind readers that faith is not about perfection but about trust and perseverance.

Through vivid storytelling, Page shares moments of divine intervention, healing, and guidance. His journey is a reminder that miracles are possible and that God's love is ever-present, even in the most challenging circumstances. This book is a beacon of hope for anyone seeking to deepen their faith or understand the impact of a life devoted to God.

Reviewed by Carol Thompson for Readers' Favorite

Tell Them I'm Real by Arnold V Page motivates us to hear the voice of God and follow His will in our darkest hours. Christians of every denomination will find something appealing in Arnold's compelling story about his search for God. This book will also bring Christianity closer to non-Christian readers. Written with a touch of dry humor, the memoir has dramatic twists and turns that keep us focused on the often miraculous events Arnold describes. This thought-provoking book witnesses the reality of God in a powerful manner.

Reviewed by Nino Lobiladze for Readers' Favorite

Tell Them I'm Real is for anyone wanting to step out into a miraculous walk with God, and I would heartily recommend it to all young pastors at the start of their training or ministry.

Joy Vee, Christian Author and Publisher.

It took me from laugh-out-loud episodes to shedding heart-breaking tears of sorrow, and moments of total wonder along the way. This is one of my favourite books from this year.

Rachel Yarworth, Author and Blogger

Books for Life Today ™

86A Totteridge Lane, High Wycombe, HP13 7PN, England
Website: https://booksforlife.today
Email: sales@booksforlife.today

Acknowledgements

I wrote this book:

- to honour my heavenly Father for the many astonishing miracles with which he has blessed me and my family in a long and eventful life,
- to convince readers who don't yet believe in God of his reality, so that they too can come to know him personally,
- and to encourage those who already walk with him to believe for miracles of their own, so that they can share God's reality and love with others more effectively.

I want to give especial thanks to the Kingdom Story Writers, who persuaded me to write this book, and in particular to Rachel Yarworth (https://rachelyarworthwriter.uk) who did such a brilliant job of editing it that you might actually want to read it to the end. In addition, I am grateful to Anna Velykorodnyy for her clinically thorough proofreading, in spite of her obsession with Oxford commas!

I'd like to thank everyone who has taught me about God and has helped me along my very slow journey to faith—so many people in so many different ways!—and especially my late wife Ann, for her unfailing encouragement and belief in me, and for introducing me more than anyone else to the realm of the supernatural.

Arnold V Page, High Wycombe, 2025

Whoever is wise, let him give heed to these things; let men consider the steadfast love of the Lord. Psalm 107:43

Contents

Prologue

It was Friday April 14th 2023, when I received an early morning phone call from my doctor.

"I have the results of your blood test," he told me. "A PSA level of 6 or 7 is normal for men of your age. Your PSA level is 47. I'm sorry."[1]

Further tests confirmed that I was indeed suffering from prostate cancer. 95% of my prostate gland was cancerous, with a disease that kills 12,000 men a year in the United Kingdom.

The following morning, I was having breakfast with my sister and her husband, prior to travelling with them for a short holiday we had booked together. As we talked at the kitchen table, some words popped into my head: *'I shall not die but live, and recount the deeds of the Lord.'* I had an idea that the words came from a psalm,[2] one of many songs in the Bible, but they weren't very familiar to me. And they had interrupted our conversation. Was God speaking to me?

After breakfast, we drove to our destination, a beautiful Christian holiday and retreat centre on the north Devon coast. In the afternoon we went for a walk in the grounds. Along a woodland path we came to a grotto cut out of the rock. While the other two waited outside, I went in to look around. There was nothing much to see, except a plaque on the wall. In the dim light I read, *'I shall not die but live, and recount the deeds of the Lord.'* This had to be more than coincidence! I felt that God was saying to me, "I really mean it!"

I did live, just as the words had said I would. After 37 sessions of radiotherapy, a further PSA blood test returned a reading of <0.01! I had been healed, as God had promised.

---

[1] PSA stands for Prostate Specific Antigens.

[2] Psalm 118:17

So now I had to do my part. Somehow, I had to recount the deeds of the Lord.

In the early summer of 2024, I attended a retreat in the wilds of the Llŷn Peninsular in north-west Wales. The retreat, attended by some forty other writers, was led by six lovely ladies who called themselves Kingdom Story Writers.[3]

I now felt well enough to write another book, and I had the idea of explaining the Christian faith in a new way to university students. It was to be called *Gateway to Eternity*. But when I shared this idea with the leaders, they advised me instead to write an account of all the things God had done in my life. This was unexpected, considering that it was the first time they had ever met me! But I believed they were in touch with the Spirit of God, and I was prepared to take their advice. Furthermore, it was precisely what my beloved late wife had urged me to do—something I had totally forgotten. So it was settled: I was to 'recount the deeds of the Lord' by writing a book!

There were six talks that week. I think it was after the final one that we were all asked to be quiet and listen to God. As soon as I did this, some words came clearly into my head, but this time they were not from the Bible. *"Tell them I'm real,"* is what I heard. It was a clear command from God. In my book, I was to tell people that there really is a God who made them, who loves them, who wants them to know and love him personally, and who can meet their deepest needs, not only for this life but for ever.

So as you read on, it's my heartfelt desire that you too may come to know God as your heavenly Father and his Son Jesus as your true friend forever.

---

[3] https://kingdomstorywriters.wordpress.com

Chapter 1. Is God Real?

The air raid sirens sound again, and my mother's fear is
communicated to me. For years I shall feel that same fear, whenever
the sirens wail.
I am being pushed, but I don't want to move. It's not safe. I am
safe in here.
Something hard is hurting my head now. I don't like it. It is
pulling me. I don't want to be pulled. I want to stay where I am.
Stop! Stop hurting me!
Suddenly, I am sliding into space.
Where am I?
I can hear voices I don't know, loud voices, so, so loud!
I feel different, exposed, and cold. I force my eyes open to see what
has happened.
Blinding light. White walls. Giant people.
I don't like it! My head hurts.
I burst into tears of angry protest.
I have been born!

※ ※ ※ ※ ※ ※ ※

"Dear God," Ivy prayed, "if you will help me to bring this child
to birth safely, I will give him back to you to be your special
servant all his life."

It was 1942. Germany's Luftwaffe was bombing London
where my mother, Ivy Stella Page, was in labour giving birth to
me, her first child. Her first two pregnancies had unhappily
terminated in miscarriages.

My mother told me much later how difficult my birth had
been. It took three days, and in the end the hospital staff used
forceps to drag me out. I was so black and blue with the
bruising that the staff wouldn't let her see me for three days.
How times have changed!

Over the next six years, my mother gave birth again, producing two dear sisters. But whether I ever got over the ordeal of my birth is not so clear! For years and years, I struggled to get out of bed each morning. "I don't want to come out. It's safe in here…"

🌿 🌿 🌿 🌿 🌿 🌿 🌿

I must have been about six years old when a lady who had lived in China came to talk to us in the Sunday school at Belmont Hall, Harrow. She explained that Chinese people didn't use letters to write, like we do, but little pictures. And she drew a stick man on a blackboard to show us the Chinese word for a man. Then she added an oval on the man's chest and said it was now the word for a woman, because women have a bosom. That, and only that, is what stuck in my little six-year-old mind from her talk. But God had introduced me to the concept of a Christian foreign missionary.

When I was eight years old, we moved to Reading. My mother decided that my sister and I should attend a Sunday school, so she took us to a different church on three successive Sundays to find one that we all liked. At the Gospel Hall, a lady swooped upon us, urging us all to sign up as 'White Ribboners' and pledge ourselves never to drink alcohol. I can't remember anything about the Church of England Sunday school we visited the second week. The Methodist Sunday school, which we visited the third week, was not only the nearest, but the one where I cried least, so that is where we went. I must have been an awful wimp when I was a child!

And so, on the basis of some childish tears, we ended up joining the Methodist Church, and the future course of my life was set.

Visually handicapped himself, my father worked for the then National Institute for the Blind. After some years, he accepted a temporary post to work in Northern Ireland, and as this was a long way from the rest of us, we communicated with him using machines called Emidictas. These were like record players, except that they used plastic-coated paper discs on which we could record our messages before rolling them up and dispatching them in cardboard tubes in the post, to be played back on the other's machine. I was thirteen years old when I recorded a message to him:

> *"I think I might be a missionary when I grow up. I am good at foreign languages, and I like camping, so I wouldn't mind living in rough conditions. Perhaps that is what God wants me to be."*

I had only a vague idea of what a missionary actually did. Apart from drawing stick women.

Aside from my church attendance, my life was little different from that of any reasonably well-behaved young person in Britain who had no interest in God. My relationship with him was more like a still life painting than an action movie, and my journals from those teenage years are peppered with doubts and uncertainties:

> *Is prayer psychological?... I am not very Christian at the moment... I want to believe in God because I am sure that life lacks something without him, but I can think of simple explanations for all 'proofs' of his existence... I am neither happy nor satisfied with my life in its present state... Something is missing... Do I really want to be an engineer?... I hope earnestly that somewhere there is a purpose to which I can devote myself, something that I can pivot every moment of my life about, something that will bring me to life...*

I longed to step onto the stage of life as a principal actor, but I couldn't find the script.

So it wasn't until my first week at Bristol University, at the age of eighteen, that my non-existent relationship with God began to stutter into life.

Initially, I shared a study bedroom with two other students, Alan and Edward. I wasn't especially sociable, so I left them to themselves, but I was listening when another student came into the room one evening in that first week and asked Edward why he went to church.

He thought for a moment.

"It helps to break the week up," he explained. "If I didn't attend church on Sundays, every day would seem the same."

What a dreadful reason for going to church, I thought.

Then a horrible thought struck me. What if that man comes over and asks why *I* go to church? I could only reply that it's how I've been brought up.

Such a reason now seemed wholly inadequate.

Fortunately, my presence in the room was ignored, but that evening I made a decision. For the rest of the term, I would be as good a Christian as I knew how. In my limited understanding, this meant attending church twice a Sunday, and praying and reading the Bible each day. If I hadn't found a reason for attending church by the end of term, I would deliberately have nothing to do with God throughout the following term. I would not even pray. And if I discovered that I could manage my life successfully without any recourse to God, I would forget about him altogether. In the meantime, if anyone asked me why I went to church, I would tell them that I was conducting an experiment to find out. Sorted!

Or so I thought...

Do angels snigger? I can't help thinking that some of them might have been doing exactly that—in the nicest possible way, of course.

I threw myself into everything of interest that university life could offer me, as if there were no tomorrow. I joined the student Methodist Society; the University Orchestra, in which I played the cello; what is now called the Revunions Comedy Society (one way to get on stage); and the Tiddlywinks Club. Practising tiddlywinks took up a lot of time, but I was rewarded for my efforts with the University's sporting colours when I represented it in matches against teams from both Swansea and Oxford University.

Towards the end of the term, I even undertook to produce a Christmas show. All the first-year students in my hall of residence were expected to stage a show for the other students at the end of the autumn term. Rehearsals for the production took a lot of organizing and a lot of time. I bought a soprano saxophone and learned to play it in order to accompany another student who was an established jazz clarinettist. I resurrected a production that our final year class at school had put on the previous year, 'A Mediaeval Knight's Mare.' And I wrote a closing number—vocals and piano score—for the whole cast to sing, before we handed the common room over to the rest of the student body for an end-of-term party. Whitbread's Forest Brown ale was the drink of choice.

You may be wondering whether I actually did any studying. The answer is yes and no. Studying engineering was not so different from being at school. We had four lectures every weekday morning, and on three afternoons we had either a practical or a tutorial for a couple of hours. I attended all of these, but apart from writing notes during the lectures, I did no further reading or work whatsoever in that first momentous term. There was so much else going on!

However, with all those extra-curricular activities occupying my attention, I was beginning to wonder whether engineering was my overriding interest. But if not engineering, what? I can remember, as if it were only yesterday, what I was thinking towards the end of that autumn term in 1960:

I need a purpose for my life. Whatever it is, it has to be 100%. Do I want to be a world-famous engineer? Do I want to be a musician, a composer, an actor? A Christian minister or missionary? Or should I devote myself to making a lot of money, to do whatever I like? What do I like? I don't know. I really don't know.

My resolution about discovering why I went to church had been forgotten. An internal war was being waged. Again and again I went over the same argument:

> *If there is a God, a God who made me for some real and valuable purpose, then to discover and live out that purpose has to be the very best thing I can do with my life. If there is a God, I could say, "O God, please tell me why you made me and how you want me to live my life, and I will do what you tell me." And if there really is a God, he will tell me what he made me for, and I will do what he tells me to.*

> *But what if there isn't a God? What if I imagine that he tells me to do something, but it's only my imagination? What if I imagine him saying, "Give up your university course and go and live in darkest Africa."[4] I would have to go, and I'd waste my life on a figment of my warped imagination.*

> *I can do what God says only if I know, if I know with absolute certainty, that he is real. And how can I know that?*

My pursuit of God's reality was beginning in earnest.

---

[4] I know Africa is no darker than Great Britain, but I'm telling you what I thought all those years ago. In 1960 many churches were still singing, 'O'er heathen lands afar, thick darkness broodeth yet...'

Chapter 2. The Way of Surrender

My task was set: to discover whether God was real. I had read in a book a promise from the Bible: *"You will seek me and find me, when you seek me with all your heart,"* but for some reason I didn't think of seeking God in the Bible itself. It seems evident to me now that to get to know someone you can't speak to in person, you must either talk to someone else who does know them or read their autobiography. And the Bible is God's autobiography.[5] But being me, I thought I could somehow work it out by myself.

Approaching Christmas at the end of our first term, we had to sit exams in six subjects, such as the strength of materials, the theory of structures, and thermodynamics. But my mind was on other things. It echoed Job's prayer in Job 23:3: *"If only I knew where I could find God!"*

On the evening before the exams began, I was not revising. I was walking around the neighbouring streets, pleading with God to show himself so that I could entrust the rest of my life to him. Heading back to my hall of residence, I walked up the middle of the lane, happy if a car ran me over and ended the conflict. I shouted aloud to heaven, "O God, if you are there, say something! Say something, just so that I know you are real! Why won't you speak to me? Why won't you speak to me? I hate you!"

I can imagine God in heaven having a word that moment with his chief archangel.

"You hear that, Gabriel? He believes in me now!"

"It doesn't sound like that to me, telling you he hates you."

"But that's the point, Gabby. He wouldn't hate me if he didn't believe in me."

---

[5] *'All scripture is inspired by God.'* 2 Timothy 3:16.

I was now sharing a room with only one other undergraduate, Tony Walker. We were both relatively quiet and undemonstrative young men, so he stared at me in astonishment when I came in late that evening and kicked the waste paper basket across the room in a fit of violent temper. I hated, yes, I hated the God who wouldn't speak to me, the God in whom I didn't believe, or at least, the God in whom I thought I didn't believe.

On the last day of term, an older student, David Hess, hesitatingly told me about a three-day Methodist Society retreat arranged in the week before the spring term began. I must have stopped going to Methsoc activities because this was news to me. He said it would be an opportunity for fellowship with other students and a chance to draw nearer to God. Of course, I immediately agreed to go: perhaps at last I would find the God I was looking for. Or perhaps he would find me?

I don't remember the name of the conference centre where we met, but I do remember feeling extremely unhappy and out of things. One evening, there was a social event. When a dance was announced, I appointed myself master of the record player, so that I wouldn't have to dance, but before long I couldn't cope even with that. I abandoned the record player and fled to my bedroom.

I had picked up from the bookstall a book with the engaging title *Practical Prayer*,[6] and I now decided to read it. Surprisingly, it wasn't all about prayer. The first chapter was about 'New Life and Higher Laws', and the second was about 'The Way of Surrender'.

What grabbed my attention most was the author's words about Jesus's first meeting with his disciples after his resurrection.

---

[6] *Practical Prayer*. Hugh Redwood, Hodder & Stoughton, 2nd edition, 1952.

As their doubts and fears must have melted away in that breath of certainty, so do we ask that our belief may be confirmed and our unbelief assisted. Our belief may go no further than the minimum with which prayer is possible, acceptance of the fact of God and an assurance that he may be found by diligent seeking; even at that it may be none too strong: but with the breath of God upon it, it will live and it will grow.

Those words, which now sound so old-fashioned, expressed just how I felt. Here was a writer who understood that believing in God is not always easy. Yes, we have to believe in God in order to pray to him, but a belief as tenuous as clinging on with our fingertips will be sufficient. Our hold on him will grow more secure as we persevere.

Jesus's first disciples—or his apprentices, as I like to call them—would not have doubted God's existence, but they did have massive doubts believing that their beloved teacher had really been the Son of God as he'd claimed, once he was crucified, dead and buried. Yet everything changed on the Sunday evening following his death, when Jesus, gloriously alive once more, met them in an upper room where they were hiding from the Romans, showed them the still unhealed scars on his wrists and side, and even ate some fish in their presence to prove he wasn't a ghost!

Distantly, dimly, more like the echo of a sound than the sound itself; more like the shadow of something than the object itself; almost unnoticed, a thought crept into my head. If Jesus did rise from the dead, as all the historical evidence testified; and if he was the Son of God, as his resurrection appeared to prove he was, then God himself must exist, for Jesus couldn't be the son of a non-existent God.

I read on to the end of that life-changing chapter.

You come with Jesus—wonderful thought—to his Father and ours. You place your all at the Father's disposal, and so give him a life in which his name may be hallowed, and a channel through which his love may be shed abroad. And you enter the kingdom, praying for its extension.[7]

My own 'way of surrender' had come. The only way to know for certain that a parachute works is to jump out of the aircraft.

I knelt at my bedside and prayed: "O God, I still don't know for certain whether you exist, but from this moment onwards, I am going to live in the belief that you do exist, and I will do whatever you tell me."

I was filled with a deep sense of peace. My battle to believe was over. I had chosen to believe.

I didn't expect to hear any immediate voice from heaven, but I resolved that when I did, I would do my best to keep my promise, wherever this might lead me. 'There is only one safe rule,' Redwood wrote: 'surrender all.' That is what I had just done.

※ ※ ※ ※ ※ ※ ※

On my return to Wills Hall for the start of the spring term, I was a changed person. I had a new love for my fellow students: I now looked forward to the opportunity of talking to someone, anyone, over the evening meal each day, instead of sitting at the table feeling the odd one out. When I walked across the neighbouring downs, all the colours of nature around me were bright and beautiful. I felt light, as though some weight had been removed from me. I thought it might be like falling in love.[8]

---

[7] Ibid.

[8] It intrigues me that although I was evidently 'born again', as Redwood had written about in the first chapter of his book, I had not repented of my sins in any traditional way, nor had I understood that only Jesus's death and resurrection had made my new birth possible. These things came later, in God's good time. We are all different, and he deals with each of us in a way that he chooses, in any way that we make possible.

During that first fortnight of my new life, the Lord answered every request I made of him, sometimes almost immediately. It was as though he was reassuring me that he really was there. One lunch hour, I wanted to go into Victoria Methodist Church to pray, but all the doors appeared to be locked. I prayed, "O Lord, please help me to find somewhere else to pray." I returned to the street, where I immediately met a fellow engineer, Mike Starr, who was walking past.

"Hello," he said. "What have you been doing?"

"I was trying to get into the church, but the door is locked."

"No, it isn't," he replied. (How did he know? He didn't attend that church.) "I'll show you."

We walked back to the side door. Mike turned the handle, gave the door a firm push, and it opened.

Another day, I asked the Lord for some way to serve him in my hall of residence. Within an hour, a notice went up asking for a volunteer to prepare the bread and wine for the monthly service of Holy Communion in the chapel.

One near miracle (in my eyes at least) had also occurred: on the first day back in Bristol after Christmas, I made my way with some trepidation to the notice board in the Engineering Building to see the exam results. Despite everything, I had come first among the thirty mechanical engineering students! Among all 120 first-year engineers, I was beaten by only one other student, who admitted to me that he spent almost all his time studying.

Looking back, I am amazed at how God enabled me to achieve those exam results while I was more occupied with seeking him. It was an awesome case of, *"Seek first his kingdom and his righteousness, and all these things shall be yours as well."* (Matthew 6:33)

Tell Them I'm Real

Chapter 3. A Night Ride

Bristol University was eighty miles from our home in Reading, and on leaving school, the question of my travelling costs had arisen. My mother travelled on a moped to a primary school where she worked as the school secretary. 'Daffodil' was a 50 cc blue French moped. She had no gears, a top speed of 25 mph on the level, and had to be helped up hills by pedalling. She was fuelled by a mixture of petrol and oil for her 2-stroke engine. My mother decided I would need something similar to get me from Reading to Bristol, and to travel around Bristol itself. So that summer, we visited a moped dealer. I rode home as the proud owner of 'Hyacinth', a twin sister for Daffodil.

One Sunday afternoon the following April, I was returning to Bristol for the start of the summer term. As usual, I had left things rather late, and by the time Hyacinth and I approached Calne in Wiltshire, it was almost dark. It had been pouring with rain, and I was soaked. I saw flashing lights ahead, and I found myself at a roadblock.

A caped policeman stopped me.

"I'm sorry, sir. You can't go on any further. The road ahead is flooded."

"I need to get to Bristol," I replied. "I've got lectures in the morning. Is there any other way I can get there?"

"If you take that road to the left, you might find a way through, sir," he said. "That's the only thing I can suggest."

I took his advice and set off along the unknown road. I had no map with me, and there were no mobile phones in those days, so I didn't know where it would lead. None of the cars that had been stopped were accompanying me, which I thought was rather strange. But at least it had stopped raining.

Then further trouble struck. A mile or two along the road, Hyacinth's single headlamp went out. Apart from her rear light, we were in total, total darkness.

"Oh God, please help me and show me what to do," I prayed.

Only four months earlier, I had been trying to decide whether I believed in God. Now, it seemed that he wanted to reassure me again that he was real, and was with me. Half a minute later, the clouds moved aside, and a bright, full moon shone down. The night lit up, and I could see where I was going again!

However, after another few miles a new problem arose as Hyacinth sputtered to a halt. She had run out of fuel. Now I was worried. How would I ever reach Bristol that night? I had never skipped a lecture, and I dreaded missing some essential lesson and being unable to catch up. This was serious!

I felt I had no choice but to continue on foot, wheeling Hyacinth along the road and somehow hoping for the best. And then the best turned up. I saw a garage ahead with two petrol pumps. My hopes lifted: rescue was at hand! Relieved, I arrived at the garage, only to find it was closed for the night! I knew life could be like a rollercoaster but this was getting ridiculous!

Dejected, I stood there, wondering what to do.

And then a remarkable change came over me. I realised I would not get to Bristol that night, and I somehow simply accepted the fact. I didn't know what would happen instead, but whatever it was, I was going to treat it as an adventure. The Lord God was with me, and he was in control. Suddenly, I felt quite excited!

I noticed a house next to the garage, and thought that perhaps the proprietor might live in it. So I rang the doorbell to find out. A lady came to the door, and she was indeed one of the proprietors. I explained the situation, and she agreed to put a coat on and come out to unlock a pump for me. Relief!

"Which kind of petrol do you want?" she asked.

"2-stroke, please."

"Oh, I'm so sorry! We've run out of 2-stroke!"

The rollercoaster went on! Undeterred, I thought for a moment. "If you have some oil, I could try mixing it with petrol in the tank."

"All right. Let's try that," she replied.

Five minutes later, Hyacinth and I were cheerfully back on the road again, our way still illuminated by a cold, bright moon. I wondered if it would provide enough light to repair a puncture, for I guessed that a puncture might be the next item on the agenda!

A sign said that the road led to Melksham. It would be far too late to look for lodging by the time I got there, but I thought that if I could find the police station, they might let me spend the night in a cell. I rather fancied the idea of being able to say I'd spent a night in a police cell.

However, God had other ideas. Before long, I came to a house with a 'Bed and Breakfast' sign. It was late, but surely it was worth trying. Thankfully, the landlady was still awake. I related my sorry plight to her, and she said I was welcome to stay the night. I slept soundly in a comfortable double bed.

Early the following morning, a knock on my bedroom door woke me up. The landlady came in.

"How did you sleep?" she asked. "You said you wanted to wake up at seven, so I've brought you a cup of tea and a newspaper."

"Thank you!"

"And I'll charge you a reduced bill, in view of the circumstances."

God's kindness was continuing.

The morning was dry and bright as I resumed my journey. The severity of the previous day's flooding was evident. Water was up to the crossbars of two rugby goalposts, while several abandoned cars were submerged almost to their roofs.

It must have been towards 10:00 a.m. when I finally reached my hall of residence. I decided that once I had sorted myself out and picked up my files, I would have time to drive down to the Engineering Building and attend at least the last two lectures of the morning.

The porter spotted me heading for my room.

"Good morning, sir. You're early today."

What? Was old Mr Hodgkinson being sarcastic? Sarcasm was entirely out of character for him.

"What do you mean?" I asked.

"Well, sir, being as it's the May Bank Holiday, I imagine most of the gentlemen won't be returning until this evening!"

While nothing that happened on the previous day would be termed miraculous, having all my needs met alone on an unknown road without any means of communication and with a moped that had neither a functioning headlamp nor petrol, was to my mind a clear demonstration of God's care for me. Following my initial prayer for help, it was another reassurance of his reality.

Chapter 4. Introducing Ann

Born in Wolverhampton, Ann Law was a special lady who would open the door to the most exciting adventure of our lives. I was told about her before I met her, and was intrigued by what I heard...

Ann was the first member of her working-class family to attend university. Her mother's great ambition for her was to return as a qualified teacher and teach in Wolverhampton High School for Girls for the rest of her working life.

She entered Bristol University a year after me to read history, with Latin as a subsidiary subject. A devout churchgoer, she began to attend both morning and evening services at the University's Anglican Church in Clifton, Bristol. Then one day, something remarkable happened.

It was Sunday, 26th November, 1961—five Sundays before Christmas. This Sunday is known in traditional Anglican churches as 'Stir Up Sunday' because of the prayer or 'collect' which is said on that particular morning:[9]

Stir up, we beseech thee, O Lord, the wills of thy faithful people; that they, plentifully bringing forth the fruit of good works, may of thee be plenteously rewarded; through Jesus Christ our Lord. Amen.

While the Reverend Canon Jeremiah Heathcote, Vicar of St Paul's and the Anglican chaplain to the University, read out this simple prayer in the morning service that Sunday, somehow

---

[9] Perhaps it was first known as Stir Up Sunday because it came at the time when people were making their Christmas puddings, and perhaps Archbishop Cranmer, who wrote the prayer book, cleverly converted it into a prayer for that day using the words 'stir' and 'fruit'.

Ann's spirit suddenly burst into life. She was filled with faith, joy, and love for the Lord, and she couldn't contain it!

Ann never told me quite how her conversation with the chaplain proceeded that morning, but she said enough for me to imagine how it might have proceeded.

[Scene: St Paul's Church, Clifton, Sunday 26th November 1961. The congregation is taking its leave of the vicar following morning worship.]

"Goodbye, vicar. Thank you very much for the service."

"Most kind. God be with you, my dear."

"Thanks. Interesting sermon."

"I'm glad you liked it."

"*Reverend Heathcote, Reverend Heathcote, something wonderful happened to me in the service!*"

"That's good. God bless you today, Mrs. Wakefield."

"*No, I must tell you. It happened during the collect.*"

"I'll see you at the church council meeting on Thursday, vicar."

"Very good, Simon."

"*Please listen to me, Reverend Heathcote. Something has happened to me. I'm so happy.*"

"Well, of course I'm pleased to hear that. Nice to see you again in church, John. Are you well now?"

"*But what has happened to me?*"

(Turning to Ann.) "It sounds as though you've had a wonderful emotional experience, my dear. I'm glad of that. But don't rely too much on emotions. Emotions don't last forever. Faith in the teachings of the church and the Holy Bible is the surest foundation for our life."

That afternoon, Ann reported her disappointment to her friend Janet Williams.

"I know something special has happened to me. But Heathcote didn't seem to know what I was talking about."

"Why don't you speak to our Methodist chaplain, Peter Morley? He's very nice, and I'm sure he'll understand. He's preaching this evening. Come to church with me, and we can talk to him about it afterwards."

And that is what they did.

≈ ≈ ≈ ≈ ≈ ≈ ≈

Rev. Peter Morley listened to Ann's story, and he told her that in his opinion she had been born again. Such an awakening of our spirit to God's forgiveness and love usually follows only after we ask Jesus to be our Saviour and Lord, but whatever had happened, it was more than a fleeting emotional experience. Only two weeks after her encounter with God, Ann applied to the United Society for the Propagation of the Gospel to be a missionary in India! That young lady had committed her life to God's service, lock, stock and barrel. Somewhat to her disappointment, they advised her to complete her degree course first and then re-apply if she still felt called to serve God overseas.

Ann began to attend the evening services at the University Methodist Church, and before long she joined the weekly Methodist Bible study group which Janet attended. And that's how my future wife became a Methodist.

I had joined the hundred-strong Methodist Society in my first week at Bristol the year before, and that's how I came to know Janet Williams. Janet soon told me about Ann's amazing experience on Stir Up Sunday, and perhaps she was match-making, for she also told me that Ann was expected to get a first in her subsidiary subject of Latin. Both items sparked my interest, and after Ann joined the Methodist church choir, singing at the front of the church on Sunday evenings, I was able to get a good look at her.

Not too tall for me, she was a slim young lady with brown hair. She had a snub nose and invitingly kissable lips! So soon after Ann joined Janet's Bible study group, I transferred from the one I was in to join hers. Going slowly was not my way of doing things when they were this important. I can still recall her look of delighted surprise the first evening that I turned up. It appeared that our attraction was mutual!

One thing that I loved about Ann was her 100% enthusiasm for anything that she enjoyed. Her eyes would shine with excitement at anything I suggested that she liked the sound of. So I had no difficulty in persuading her that our first date should be a picnic beside Chew Magna Lake, to the south of Bristol, on St Valentine's Day, February 14th, 1962!

By this time, my moped Hyacinth had been replaced by a 150 cc motorbike that I unimaginatively named James, James being its make. I remember so well the clothes Ann wore that day, cuddling up close behind me on the saddle: a thick orange roll neck sweater and some dark blue trousers that strapped under her feet. Her white crash helmet was so much smaller than my great grey racing helmet!

The day was frosty but sunny. I discarded my old motorcycling jacket in favour of a somewhat loosely-knitted green jumper that my sister had made for me, and after lunch I picked Ann up for the 10-mile journey to Chew Magna, guided by an Esso roadmap. We enjoyed our special picnic together by the deserted lake and set off back to Bristol in the last of the daylight.

As the sun went down, it became cold, so very cold! My sister's jumper was altogether inadequate to protect me from the bitingly cold rush of air against me. My woollen-gloved hands were numb. I was too dangerously cold to take Ann back to her hall of residence as well as mine, so we headed for my hall of residence and went to the room of my friend David Hess. It was the sole student room in Wills Hall that had an electric fire. Ann had to explain why we had come: my mouth was so frozen I couldn't speak! As we thawed out and the circulation returned to our frozen limbs, the pain was intense.

Only a madman would have suggested a picnic in the middle of February. And only a mad woman would cheerfully have accompanied him. But by then we were both madly in love!

Tweezy, gurgle,
lilac eyes.
Mischief twinkling up at me.
Hug a shrug
and squeeze my hand:
run off light and don't come back.
Mocking sorry
twingy twangy
hide your eyes with little fingers
Fling your arms around to kiss me
kiss away
a load of thought.
Gooble, gurble,
sunny pavement.
I'm in love with Ann.

If our first date didn't convince you that I was mad, the way in which I tried to propose to Ann will almost certainly do the trick. I decided to propose marriage to her on the summit of Mount Snowdon on the stroke of midnight on New Year's Eve, December 1962.

I had learned my lesson about frostbite, and I did not intend driving 240 miles to North Wales in the heart of winter on my motorbike.

Bill Geers, the student president of the University's Methodist Society and a PhD engineering student, drove a small Austin van. I asked Bill if he would be willing to drive us to Snowdonia. I said he was welcome to bring a girlfriend with him, but having no girlfriend of his own, I invited my sister Geraldine to make up a foursome. Both Bill and Geraldine knew my intention, but Ann, of course, did not. [10]

---

[10] As a result of this expedition, Bill and Geraldine fell in love and married. They now have four children, numerous grandchildren and even some great grandchildren. Probably none of these people would exist today if Bill had not owned a small blue Austin van.

We stayed at Llanberis youth hostel. Some members of the Scout troop that I still belonged to were also staying there, and it was the knowledge that they would be around if we got into difficulties that had persuaded my parents to allow my sister to accompany Ann, Bill and me.

On New Year's Eve, the four of us wrapped up as warmly as possible and set off for the five-mile climb to the summit of Yr Wyddfa, then known as Snowdon. It wasn't long before we were treading through thick snow.

The higher we climbed, the harder the wind blew, until at one point Bill and Geraldine were almost blown off their feet. Some other climbers coming down met us and advised us not to go any further: it was far too dangerous.

Reluctantly, on my part at least, we retraced our steps. It wasn't yet midnight, so I asked Bill to drive us along the edge of Llyn Peris, a lake near Llanberis. We came to a small building like a little ruined castle at the water's edge. Asking Bill to stop, I invited Ann to step outside with me. I led her into the 'castle'. An almost full moon was shining down on us.

"Ann," I said, peering at my watch, "It's midnight. I wish you a happy New Year. Will you marry me?"

Her eyes sparkled in the reflected light of the moon. "Arnold, your timing is perfect," she replied. "Of course I will."

Our kiss was very special.

This was not quite the end of the story. We all returned to the youth hostel and, of course, we discovered that we were locked out. Sometimes I am so bad at thinking ahead! I threw some tiny stones at the window of what I believed was the men's dormitory where the Scouts were sleeping, in the hope of waking someone to let us in. Unfortunately, it was not the right window: it was the window of the lady warden's bedroom! In her dressing gown and hair curlers, she opened the front door for us, extremely annoyed. Unmoved by our romantic excuses, she confiscated our youth hostel membership cards and refused to return them until we had all paid a fine!

There's a verse in the Bible that says God orders all things according to the counsel of his will. I believe he was looking after us that night, because the returning climbers' advice to turn back, and finding the little ruined 'castle' by the lake on the exact stroke of midnight as a romantic alternative to Snowdon, saved us from both danger and disappointment.

What is so strange is that some years afterwards I returned to Llyn Peris and I could find no trace of the little 'castle', nor of any space between the lake and the road where it might have been located!

Tell Them I'm Real

Chapter 5. An Early Test of Obedience

I was sitting on the floor in my third-year room in a dilemma about my future. Did I want to spend the rest of my life as an engineer, or as something else altogether? My final degree exams would begin in another two weeks, but try as I might, my mind rebelled at the thought of revising. What was wrong with me? Didn't I want to pass?

I had prayed for help, but no help had come. Why wasn't God answering?

[Monday, April 29th, 1963]

Maybe praying doesn't help because I don't feel I can fully serve God as an engineer. But to do anything else and waste three years of study would be ridiculous. Am I to go through my whole life doing work that I feel is of no use to him? Does he want me to do something different? One thing I'm sure about: I remain determined to do whatever he wants me to do. Whatever it is, I know I shall never be happy unless I do his will.

So I sat on the floor and thought about the kind of person God had made me, at least as I saw myself. Every consideration, one after another, seemed to point to the fact that God wanted me to be a Christian minister! The moment I reached that inescapable conclusion, I didn't rejoice: I rebelled!

I can't do this. I can't. I'm hopeless at making speeches. I don't love people. I haven't even any faith in God. And as for speaking to a woman whose husband has just died, I wouldn't know where to start.

I felt sure that God wanted me to be a minister, and I was equally sure he had made a mistake. For almost a week, I argued with him. Perversely, I was then able to do a small amount of revision for the exams. And then it was announced in church that a half-day conference had been arranged for young men[11] who were considering entering the ministry, to take place the following Saturday. Of course I went!

The conference didn't help me much, but afterwards I went into the main building of the church to pray. I knelt and said, *"O God, I'm still sure you are making a mistake, but I'll do it if you want me to. I'll leave it to the church to decide."*

The exams came and went. A few weeks later, having left university, I had to make a speech at my twenty-first birthday party. It was a disaster. I forgot what I was going to say. I went red in the face. I missed half the points I should have made, including thanking my parents. My fears were confirmed: I was hopeless at making speeches! Yet three months later, having been accepted to go on trial as a Methodist local preacher, I was being thanked for the 'wonderful' service I had taken. And a year after that, I wrote:

God is carrying out his intentions. He has given me faith in his power to save and free people from sin, and such a longing for others to know his love that last Sunday, I even found myself preaching in a Kent marketplace.

Who can imagine what God can accomplish in us when we put our lives fully in his hands?

For the record, I obtained a good degree in engineering, and my three years of studying engineering were absolutely not a waste of time, as we shall discover later in my story. God is a master planner, and when the jigsaw of our life is complete, we shall see that every piece was a part of it.

---

[11] In those days, there were no women ministers in the Methodist Church.

❧ ❧ ❧ ❧ ❧ ❧ ❧

On leaving university, I accepted a post as a graduate engineering apprentice with Vickers-Armstrongs Ltd in Swindon.

Before being accepted for training as a Methodist minister, I had to qualify as a lay preacher. I studied worship, preaching, and the Old and New Testaments, and I led church services on Sundays in the neighbouring villages. During my second year in Swindon, I pursued further studies, and took several trial services as a test of my suitability for the Methodist ministry. Being in full-time employment, I had to carry out all these studies and activities in the evenings when I was not attending night school for further engineering qualifications, and at weekends when I was not preaching or visiting Ann in Bristol.

Finally, in July 1965, I was informed by the Methodist Conference that my candidature had been successful and I could begin full-time training for the ministry in September.

I completed my apprenticeship with two weeks to spare.

"We were wondering whether it was worth increasing your salary for only two weeks," my manager told me with a smile. "In the end we decided we would, just so that you can know what you'll be missing!"

Chapter 6. A Prayer for a Cat and a Commission to Go Far

My upcoming training as a Methodist minister was based on a three-year theology degree course at Richmond College, near London, to begin in September of that year. Ann was finishing her post-graduate teacher training and would soon be looking for a teaching post. We wanted to get married before I entered college, at least a month or two beforehand, to give us time to get used to married life first.

In those days, to train for the Methodist ministry one had to be a man, not a woman, and preferably single. The college had no double bedrooms, so any married couples had to rent their own accommodation somewhere nearby. Furthermore, if a single man wished to marry before beginning his training, he required special permission from the Methodist Conference, which was not always forthcoming.

The problem was that the Conference didn't take place until late in June, so we might not know until early July whether we would receive permission to get married. What if the answer were no? Would we have to live separate lives for another three years, I in my solitary single room in college while Ann found a teaching job somewhere, returning from school each afternoon to some lonely bedsit?

If we were going to get married in mid-July, we'd have to make arrangements for the wedding long before that, which meant that an unfavourable decision would require us to cancel all the arrangements at the last moment and call the wedding off. So should we postpone our plans in any case, to avoid such a possibility?

My earlier adventure with the moped had taught me to trust God to manage things. We prayed together that he would do so again, and we went ahead and booked a wedding for July 17th. It was to be conducted in Wolverhampton by our friend and former chaplain, Peter Morley.

Merely two weeks before the wedding, Peter sent us a telegram: 'Conference approved request for marriage. Congratulations.' What a beautiful answer to our prayers! And what a relief!

After the wedding, we set off to spend our honeymoon in a tiny cottage hidden in the woods on the Lee Abbey estate in North Devon.

The sun had set that Saturday evening when we reached Porlock Hill. My little 150cc motorbike couldn't carry two riders and a big suitcase up a 1 in 4 hill. Unfortunately, my new wife couldn't ride a bicycle, let alone a motorbike, so in her brand-new going-away outfit she had to walk up Porlock Hill in the gathering darkness while I drove ahead to where it was less steep.

It was about 11:00 p.m. by the time we reached Lee Abbey, and it must have been nearly midnight before we could settle down in Tinkerbell Cottage for our first proper night together!

🌿 🌿 🌿 🌿 🌿 🌿 🌿

I had managed to rent a flat above a chemist's shop near Swindon for our first married home. The rent was only £4 a week, perhaps because we had to share our bedroom with scores of active woodworms! Our immediate tasks were to find a proper flat near Richmond and a teaching post for Ann so that we could pay for it.

Ann looked in TES, then known in full as the Times Educational Supplement, and she found an advertisement for a combined history and Latin teacher at Twickenham Grammar School, a private co-ed school not far from Richmond. She applied for the post and was duly appointed, so far as I recall merely on the basis of two shining references. Amazing!

Being the school's only history teacher, Ann straight away became a head of department, on a head of department's pay—an astonishing first post straight out of teacher training.

We soon found a tiny furnished flat in Teddington. It was within walking distance of the school for Ann, and only a three-mile motorbike ride for me to my college in Richmond. So we were all set up. Our great and mighty father God had provided for all our needs!

🌿 🌿 🌿 🌿 🌿 🌿 🌿

One day, Ann's hairdresser asked her if she would like to have a kitten. We went to the hairdresser's house, where six beautiful kittens, all of different colours, were chasing each other around the back of a settee. They were irresistible! We chose a ginger tom whom we named Rufus and brought him home to join our household.

We loved little Rufus. One day, we took him for a walk on a lead, like a dog, to nearby Bushey Park. When I let him off the lead, he ran straight up a tree. I had to ask another man to help me to get him down. Another time, we took Rufus to my parents' house in Reading, some 35 miles away, with Ann holding him on the back of my motorbike! We took him out on the River Thames in a rowing boat, and I had to restrain him from jumping out of the boat to catch some ducks on the other side of the river. We were crazy in those days!

Rufus was fearless but foolish: he seemed to believe that if he ran across a road fast enough there wouldn't be time for a car to hit him. But one Thursday in the Easter holidays, this was proved wrong. As I came out of the house, there was a screeching of brakes, a tiny howl of pain, and I saw an injured Rufus disappear down the side of a house on the other side of the main road. I ran after him while the car driver called out his apologies. I knew it was not his fault.

I found Rufus hiding behind someone's garden shed, seriously injured. I believe God was in the timing, for if I hadn't come out of our house at that exact moment, I would probably never have found him, and he would have died where he was hiding.

Rufus fought against being picked up, but with some scratches I succeeded. I carried him to the vets and left him in their care.

On the Saturday morning, I visited the surgery. The vet was a tall man with a moustache and a kind voice.

"Ah yes, your little cat. He is still very much alive, but one of his back legs is going gangrenous. I'm sincerely sorry."

"What does that mean?" I asked.

"It means we'll either have to put Rufus to sleep or amputate his leg. Most cats can manage nearly as well on three legs as on four, but the decision is up to you. If you go for amputation we could do it on Monday morning. I'm sorry I can't give you better news."

"I'd like to have a word with my wife before we decide what to do," I told him.

Glumly, I returned home.

It wasn't hard to come to a decision. I phoned the vets and asked them to proceed with the amputation.

On Saturday evening and Sunday morning, Ann and I discussed the possibility of praying about it. At our church service on Sunday, the Bible reading was about Jesus healing the servant of the Roman centurion who had total faith in Jesus's ability to heal him. We knew Jesus said that God cared about birds, so we thought, why not cats? We came home and, still hesitantly, sat together on the settee and prayed for Rufus to be healed.

On Monday afternoon, I rang the vet's to ask how the operation had gone. The receptionist answered the phone.

"The vet didn't do the amputation," she replied. "When he examined the leg this morning, he found it wasn't gangrenous after all. I'm not quite sure what happened there. However, it will probably be necessary to remove your cat's two middle toes. The vet is busy at the moment, but he'll give you a call when he's free."

Do cats have toes? That's what I wrote in my diary. I'm not sure now that they carried out even that operation in the end. Rufus's leg was always rather stiff after this event, but otherwise he was fine, and he had learned his lesson about how to cross a road more sensibly.

More importantly, it was our first experience of a healing miracle.

🌿 🌿 🌿 🌿 🌿 🌿 🌿

Richmond College was originally founded to train Methodists who wanted to be foreign missionaries. While specialised training for missionary work was no longer provided, the college's missionary tradition remained strong, so at the end of my second year, I was asked to consider whether I wanted to serve at home or abroad once my final year of training had been completed.

I was faced with a major decision: should I serve God in Britain or in some far-off foreign country? I needed to know God's will in this important matter, but my years in college hadn't encouraged me to believe in any supernatural guidance. So I drew up a list of pros and cons, but it didn't help. They were equal in number. What else could I do?

There was only one thing I could think of: I prayed that the Lord would lead me to an answer in my Bible. I opened it in faith that the Holy Spirit would choose where it opened, and I read the first verse that caught my eye. It was not on a familiar page.

The verse I read was from Jeremiah 23:23: *"Am I a God near at hand, says the Lord, and not a God far off?"* The Lord was telling Jeremiah that he wasn't only the God of Israel, his chosen people, but the God of foreign nations as well. For me, God was undoubtedly answering my prayer. He wanted me to serve him somewhere overseas, somewhere very distant. I had no doubt that he had spoken.

You probably think this was a foolhardy way to make a major life decision, and on a merely human level I'd have to agree with you. A less individualistic person than I would have consulted people who knew me, and perhaps other people who had themselves served God abroad. But I had once told God that I would do whatever he told me, and I wanted him, not other people, to tell me what he wanted.

Nevertheless, while I was writing this memoir, I was interested to know whether I could have come upon such a verse by pure chance, or whether it was more likely to have been the result of divine guidance. So I opened the Bible at random 100 times to see how many other random verses could have answered my question. Not one single verse had any relevance to it whatsoever.

That evening, I talked to Ann about my decision. She had once wanted to go to India as a missionary, so the idea of working abroad was no problem for her. But we decided it would be best for me to gain some practical experience first by serving my first appointment in England. Meanwhile, for my final year's special subject, I chose West African Religions, in case the Lord called us to Africa. Somehow, Africa no longer appeared to be so dark as I had once childishly thought.

At the end of my three years of 'training', during which I learned Greek, church history, philosophy of religion and other such things, but next to nothing about the practical and pastoral aspects of leading a church, I was appointed to a probationary minister's post in what to me were the semi-foreign wilds of Norfolk. I began my ministry on September 1st, 1968. The initial appointment was for three years.

Chapter 7. When the Spirit Comes

The manse, which was to be our home for the next three years at least, was an old 4-bedroomed detached house with a large garden. It was heated—or would be in the winter—by coal fires, with coal that I would have to bring in each morning from its storage in a former outside toilet. None of the windows was double-glazed. We were close to the North Sea, and I didn't look forward to the winter!

One of the first services of Holy Communion[12] that I took was in the nearby hamlet of Wickmere. Its adult population was a mere 132 persons, and so far as I remember, the chapel's congregation numbered no more than six.

The Methodist Service Book had two versions of the order of service for Holy Communion. In college we had been encouraged to use the fuller one. Both versions included prayers for the congregation to say, but I couldn't see any service books in the Wickmere chapel. Trying to be sensitive, I asked the chapel steward which version of the Holy Communion service they preferred.

"We don't use books here," he said. "You do it."

There was probably more to this than saving money by not buying service books. Many years earlier, there had been a spiritual revival in the area, a time when the fear of God had come upon many people, and they flocked to the chapels and churches seeking forgiveness for their sins and committing

---

[12] Holy Communion or The Lord's Supper is a special service or ceremony based on Jesus's instructions to his disciples at their last meal together before his crucifixion. He broke some bread, gave pieces of it to them, and told them to remember his broken body whenever they ate it; then he gave each of them some wine to drink and asked them to remember his blood shed for them whenever they drank it.

their lives to the service of Jesus.[13] At such a time, formal worship with service books would have been irrelevant.

Some of the oldest members of my churches had lived through that time in their youth. One of these was Richard Keeler. He was 100 years old when I visited him in hospital. He had been born in 1869, in the middle of Queen Victoria's reign!

"Mr Keeler is a dear man," one of the nurses told me. "He's always asking us, 'Are you on the right road?'"

I found his bed, sat on a chair beside it, and introduced myself. After a bit, Mr Keeler reached towards me as best he could and stretched out his hand above my head.

"May God bless your ministry," he said. "May you see souls saved in your time. May the Holy Spirit anoint you with words of truth and love and power that will bear fruit, fruit that will abide."

It was awesome! I felt as though I had been blessed by one of the ancient patriarchs like Abraham or Moses.

※ ※ ※ ※ ※ ※ ※

Ann and I had wasted no further time starting a family, and in November 1968, our first child was born. I was so thrilled, I made up three songs in three days to celebrate his birth. We named our lovely little boy Julian.

At the same time, I was discovering that being a church leader was more challenging than I had expected. We'd all like life to be a garden of roses, but in this imperfect world, that inevitably means there will also be many thorns. God himself is full of truth and love, but that isn't always true of those who claim to be his children.

I wrestled with the impossible expectations of being a probationary minister in charge of ten churches; chairing business meetings in each of them; leading weeknight meetings for home missons, overseas missions and, in several of them,

---

[13] I have reimagined this revival, based on what records I could find, in a blog https://www.booksforlife.today/blog/index.php?the-last-leaf

harvest festival auctions; overseeing the accounts in some of the smaller churches; visiting members in their homes; and continuing with further probationary studies.

The following year, I wrote about my struggles to our former university chaplain, with whom Ann and I had kept in touch.

[Friday, May 23rd, 1969: letter to Rev Peter Morley]

With ten chapels to look after and three services to take every Sunday, the appointment is entirely unsuitable for a probationer. There are deep family divisions in my main church. In the second largest church, there is resentment that they no longer have a minister stationed there as they did previously. Collections are the all-important register of success. Membership has been dropping rapidly in the last few years. The leaders of one more spiritually alive church are planning to leave en masse to join another denomination. We both feel spiritually empty. We long to possess more of the Holy Spirit, his gifts and fruit. They are needed very much here.

In Paul's letter to the church in Galatia, found in the Bible, he listed what he called the fruit of the Spirit—the character of someone who is filled with the Spirit of God. '*Now the fruit of the Spirit is love, joy, peace, patience, kindness, goodness, faithfulness, gentleness, self-control.*' (Galatians 5:22,23) I found myself thinking about this passage, and I asked myself:

"Do I have love for the people I am ministering to? Not really. It's a job God has given me, but not one I am especially enjoying. How about joy? Decidedly not joy. I don't feel at all joyful. Peace? No: all kinds of anxieties."

One by one, I crossed off in my mind every single one of those nine fruits of the Holy Spirit that Paul had listed in his letter. I was left with an inevitable conclusion: if these characteristics were the fruit of the Holy Spirit, I needed the Holy Spirit!

After his resurrection and after spending another six weeks with his disciples, the risen Jesus told them that he had to go back to heaven, but they were to wait in Jerusalem for a gift from God—the gift of the Holy Spirit.

Sure enough, on the Jewish feast of Pentecost, the Spirit fell in extraordinary power upon all 120 disciples. A mighty wind shook the building, and flames of fire appeared over their heads. They spontaneously began praising God, but in a whole variety of foreign languages. The crowds who had travelled to Jerusalem for the feast from many different countries heard them speaking in their own languages. And when Jesus's disciple Peter explained to them from the Scriptures what it was all about, 3000 men committed their lives to Jesus that day as their promised Saviour and Lord.

It was an extraordinary event, an event which has since been regarded as the birth of the Christian Church. And since both Jesus and Peter had promised that God would give his Holy Spirit to any of his followers who asked him, I began to ask for myself!

For the next three months, I prayed for the Holy Spirit. But at the same time, my diary tells me that I was wrestling with my lifelong nemesis: my bed. It was a constant battle to get up each morning.

[Thursday, August 14th, 1969]

Why won't my flesh[14] lie down? O Lord, slay this sin-wrapped body and fill me with your Spirit!

[Monday, August 18th, 1969]

---

[14] 'Flesh' is a word used in the Bible for our natural physical desires to eat, drink, sleep, engage in sexual activity, etc., as distinct from our spirit, which should rightfully be in charge.

I want the Holy Spirit. I have resolved to fast on Wednesdays and Fridays.

And I wasn't the only one struggling. Ever since we had arrived in Aylsham, Ann's faith in God and her love for him had been fast disappearing. She struggled to look after our first baby, and she was constantly tired. She was an excellent schoolteacher, and she had a great knowledge of history, with an almost photographic memory, but she was not awfully practical. And raising a baby involves a lot of practical tasks.

I know now that I didn't spend nearly as much time supporting Ann as I should have done.

We couldn't go out in the evenings together because, for the first two years at least, no one in the church ever offered to help with babysitting, even when we asked. One evening, in desperation, we went out somewhere for an hour or so on our own. It seemed perfectly safe, for once little Julian was asleep for the night, he never woke until the morning. I know we shouldn't have done this, but times were different then, and as I say, we were desperate.

Where we went I don't remember, but the following day an anonymous note was pushed through our letterbox: "If you ever leave your baby alone again, I will tell the police." Who wrote it? A neighbour? Or worse, a church member? Whoever wrote it knew that we had no babysitter. So who was watching us so closely?

I feel tears come to my eyes as I relive my feelings in those difficult days.

Looking back, I should probably have admitted publicly to the congregation that we were struggling. I guess I had a picture of a minister as a strong leader on whom everyone else relied, an impossible ideal and an ungodly picture of how the members of Christ's body are meant to relate to one another. I still wasn't much good at personal relationships.

By August 1969, Ann was manifestly suffering from a postnatal depression. She had lost all her self-confidence and kept bursting into tears. Some kind friends (not in the church) had offered us a few days in their flat at the seaside, hoping it might alleviate Ann's depression. It made no difference. All her love for life had gone, and neither of us could imagine what we could do. In those days, doctors dealt mostly with physical problems, not problems like depression. It never occurred to either of us to seek the help of a doctor.

On the afternoon of August 18th, 1969, the same day that I had resolved to fast for the Holy Spirit, a minister friend was talking to us about what it meant to him to possess the Spirit. David Watkins was a Bible-believing minister in another part of the same circuit of churches.[15] Knowing about Ann's depression, he told us that evil spirits can sometimes take hold of people who are in a state of medical depression, so that the illness becomes spiritual and not merely physical.

That night, Ann and I prayed together before going to bed. About 2:30 a.m., I woke up. Unhappily restless, Ann had still not managed to sleep, and now she was keeping me awake. I escaped to the spare bedroom. It was the first time in our married life we hadn't slept together. I wanted to get some sleep, but half an hour later I was still awake, anxious and upset, my unhappy thoughts centred on the church. I heard Ann go downstairs, so I decided to join her. In the kitchen, we found something to eat together.

"O Arnold, whatever shall we do?" my wife asked me despairingly.

"I don't know. Why don't we read the Bible together? Maybe the Lord will say something to us through it."

We sat down at the table together, and I chose two passages, one from Ephesians, which reassured Ann, though not me, and then Psalm 103. I purposely chose a psalm, but the one I read was selected entirely at random... or so I thought.

---

[15] A circuit is a group of Methodist churches overseen by two or more ministers, each with particular responsibility for one or more churches within the circuit.

Bless the LORD, O my soul; and all that is within me, bless his holy name! Bless the LORD, O my soul, and forget not all his benefits, who forgives all your iniquity, who heals all your diseases, who redeems your life from the Pit, who crowns you with steadfast love and mercy, who satisfies you with good as long as you live so that your youth is renewed like the eagle's...

Psalm 103:1-5

The psalm continued along its reassuring way. In some extraordinary manner, it was as if the Lord was speaking to us directly.

I am old enough to remember writing at school with a pen and ink. If one wanted the ink to dry rapidly, one used blotting paper, a soft kind of paper that absorbed the excess ink without smudging it.

That night, it was as though we were no longer reading some dry old psalm written 1000s of years ago: it was as if the words had been freshly written just for us, imprinting themselves directly upon the blotting paper of our bruised spirits. We had heard the Lord's voice, and a miracle was about to happen.

Ann and I returned to our separate bedrooms. I was filled with gratitude to God for encouraging us so wonderfully. My heart was full of thanksgiving, and I repeated the words of the psalm as best I could remember them.

But I didn't fall asleep. Instead, I started to think again about my churches and other churches and people not in a church at all, and about people in factories I had worked in, and friends of mine who were atheists. And it seemed terribly clear to me that everyone was bound fast by powers of evil and darkness. It barely seemed possible that I would ever find rest among people set free from sin and rejoicing together in the life of the kingdom of heaven.

And then it occurred to me that such a sense of despair often came to me at the same time as a similar sense came to Ann. It felt as if Satan suddenly remembered us and sent one or two of his servants to attack us together. I wasn't sure that I believed in evil spirits, but the thought was so strong that I followed the advice our minister friend had given us that same afternoon. I repeated aloud relevant verses from God's word that I knew, so that any evil things would have to depart. I said, *"Perfect love casts out fear." "Now is the prince of this world cast out." "In the name of Jesus, I command you to depart."*

The moment I said, "In the name of Jesus, I command you to depart," I felt that Jesus's name was quite sufficient to send any evil spirits off in a great fright!

And then I thought I heard Ann crying.

I unburied my head from my pillow to listen. It sounded as though she was talking to someone. I thought, *"She must have gone to sleep quickly, and she is talking in her sleep."* It sounded as though several people were speaking. *"I know,"* I thought. *"An evil spirit possessed her, and through what I have just said, God is casting it out!"* The idea was unnerving, to say the least. I prayed, *"I praise you, Lord. Now let your Holy Spirit find a dwelling place within her and remain there, that the evil powers may never be able to return."*

(In those days, I thought I had to use somewhat formal language to address the Lord!)

Ann came into my room. She was perspiring and shaking.

"What's happened to me, Arnold?"

"It's all right," I replied. "I think an evil spirit has come out of you."

"Oh no!" she said. "It wasn't anything nasty. It was lovely!"

"Tell me about it."

"After you read from the Bible, I came back to bed again. I was thinking of those lovely words that God spoke to us. And suddenly, my mind seemed to be full of light. I began to say thank you to God, but I found I wasn't speaking in English. I didn't want to stop; I felt so happy. I kept my head under the bedclothes so I wouldn't disturb you, but then it got too loud anyway, so I sat up. It was lovely. I'd have liked to go on speaking, but I thought I'd better stop and come and tell you what happened."

There was only one thing I could say in reply: "You must have been speaking in tongues!"

Neither of us had heard of anyone outside the pages of the New Testament exercising this ability to speak in another language supernaturally. We'd read in the Bible how the first believers in Jesus were able to speak in other languages on the day of Pentecost, and how St Paul encouraged every believer to use the gift in personal prayer as a means of growing stronger in spirit. But we certainly didn't know that it happened today as well. It was as if heaven had broken into our troubled lives. Maybe an evil spirit did leave Ann, too.

At that moment, Ann's depression vanished as though it had never existed.

In the morning, I heard the most beautiful singing upstairs, more lovely than anything I had ever heard. Ann was singing in the Spirit. She soon began to have words from the Lord for us both, words in English, not other tongues, beautiful words of prophetic encouragement that spoke directly to our hearts, as well as to our minds.

A couple of days later, I met a lady in the street. She said, "I've just been talking to your wife. My goodness, she's like a different person. Your holiday has done her good!"

[Tuesday, August 19th 1969]

All the previous tenseness has gone. Ann has a completely new insight into the things of God and an authority that I don't possess. So great a change, so suddenly! We are living in the midst of a miracle that is almost too thrilling to think of. It is only tinged by a sadness we both feel that I am still waiting.

Yes, I had been praying for the Holy Spirit to come into my life, and God had answered my prayer, but it felt as though he had got the wrong person!

Tell Them I'm Real

Chapter 8. Filled with the Spirit

[Monday, August 25th, 1969]

I spent one and a half hours in prayer, mainly for the Spirit. I really can't pray well. I want to adore God, but I either go to sleep or start dreaming about my troubles. Nevertheless, after an hour, God showed me three things clearly:

I must love him and not seek his gifts for themselves. But I cannot make myself love him. Only he can give me such love.

Part of me is unwilling to be filled with the Spirit because I can see that I shall have to do some things I don't want to do. But I never will want to do them until the Spirit takes possession of me!

There is so much pride in me! Part of the reason I want the Spirit is to go up a 'spiritual class'. I dream of increased congregations, of people talking about me, and even friends with the Spirit coming to me for guidance because I am a 'learned minister'. I hate my pride. I long to desire God because of himself, not for myself. But again, it seems clear I can do nothing about it. Only when God's Spirit changes me will this dreadful pride go!

It appears there is nothing to do but to go on waiting in faith!

[Tuesday, August 26th, 1969]

Cutting his back teeth, Julian has been more trouble this last week than any in his life. Poor Ann has had periods of impatience and even flashes of temper, but thanks be to God, he sets her free when she asks him to. Previously, these moods could have lasted a day or more. She praises God in tongues every day, and the gift is certainly not a flash in the pan. But I can see now what it means in Romans

45

7 about 'the flesh striving against the spirit'. It is true, yes, that God sets us free from sin, but we still sin. The flesh rises up, triumphs for a moment, and is then conquered. It fights and hurts us, but then loses every battle!

I was thrilled about what had happened to Ann the previous week, but desperately sad that God had still not answered my prayers for myself. I fasted all day on the following Wednesday and Friday, and on the Sunday morning before church. I so longed to be filled with the Spirit myself.

I had notified my main congregation in Aylsham that I would preach that Sunday on the baptism of the Holy Spirit. I thought that the Lord might answer my prayers during the service. But instead, two wasps buzzed around throughout the service, and when I started to preach, they came and buzzed around me. One even crawled along my glasses, and I had to kill it. The poor people were quite distracted. I don't suppose they took in a single word I said.

I'd written a letter about Ann's amazing experience to our minister friend, David. He phoned me in response and strongly encouraged us to go to Perivale in Middlesex, where some friends of his were conducting a fortnight of gospel[16] meetings. He said some people there would pray for me. We agreed to go on the Friday afternoon and return on the Saturday, in time for my Sunday services that weekend.

[Tuesday, August 26th, 1969, continued]

What a joy it will be to be able to stop pretending I am a Christian, when in my heart I have always known I had neither the powers nor the fruits of New Testament Christians! At long last, I shall not need to explain away anything in the New Testament. 'O Comforter draw near! Within my heart appear, and kindle it, thy holy flame bestowing.'

---

[16] 'Gospel' means good news, 'God spelling' it out for us.

46

On Friday, August 29th, Ann, Julian and I found our way to the church hall where the 'Come Back to God Campaign' people were holding their evening meeting. And guess what? The subject of the sermon was 'The Baptism of the Holy Spirit.' It was almost word for word what I had preached the previous Sunday!

When the formal part of the meeting ended, many people asked for one-to-one prayer. The leaders enlisted me to pray for some of them. At one point, Ann was asked to help them pray for a lady who was demon-possessed. They had been unable to cast the demon out, and they needed Ann to help them with her gift of tongues, as none of them had that ability.

We went into a room where a woman was writhing about on the floor, hissing like a snake. We had never seen anything like that. The demon—for it must have been a demon—was speaking from her in a strangely deep voice. It was arguing with the minister, who was telling it to leave her. "I won't come out, I won't come out!" it said.

As soon as Ann saw the woman, she burst into a powerful, loud tongue. It was not beautiful, but it was effective! "All right, I'm coming," growled the demon. The woman immediately went quiet, and before long, she opened her eyes and stood up, calm and free!

It was nearly 2:00 a.m. when the leaders finally got round to praying for me. They'd left me until last. Three of them gathered around me, laid hands on me, and asked the Lord to fill me with his Holy Spirit. I found myself breathing in very, very deeply, trying to open my heart and spirit to the Comforter whom Jesus had promised the Father would give me when I asked. I did not speak in tongues, perhaps because none of those who prayed for me exercised that gift and so didn't expect me to exercise it either. But the fact was that afterwards, they described what happened to me as 'a mighty baptism of the Spirit'.

The next morning, during a walk in a local park with my baby son, I found myself telling an old park keeper how Jesus had died because of our sin. I'm pretty sure it was the first time I had shared the gospel with a stranger, but I didn't do it because I felt it was my duty: I did it because I wanted to!

I was so pleased about this, because one of the principal reasons I'd wanted to be filled with the Spirit was to enable me to talk about Jesus to people outside the church. It was as though God was giving me immediate, next-morning reassurance, that he had answered my prayer.

When Jesus, at the age of thirty, was baptized in water, the Holy Spirit descended upon him in the visible form of a dove. The Spirit then took Jesus off to the wilderness for six weeks to prepare for his public ministry, which was soon to begin. The devil soon got to work, trying to make him doubt what had just happened and what he had just heard, and Jesus replied to each temptation by quoting a relevant verse from the Bible.

Something similar happened to me. For several days after the visit to Perivale, I found myself doubting whether God really had filled me with his Spirit. But, like Jesus, I kept answering these doubts with the word of God: *"If you then, who are evil, know how to give good gifts to your children, how much more will the heavenly Father give the Holy Spirit to those who ask him!"* [17] I had asked my Father for the Spirit, so I was going to believe that he had kept his word, because God never lies.

The battle lasted no more than three days. I soon found that whenever I began to pray, the first words that came out of my mouth were, "I love you, Lord. I love you." It was so different from earlier, when I had found prayer such an unrewarding duty.

One extraordinary result of my baptism in the Spirit—and I'm sure it must have been a result of it—was that everything started to go well in the church. It was as if all things were at last working together for good.

---

[17] Luke 11:13

I now felt such a love for God when I prayed that words alone were inadequate. After saying, "I love you, God" seven or eight times, it began to get boring. If only I could speak in tongues, I thought, I'd be able to praise my Father properly. But every time I asked him to help me speak out words given by the Spirit, I'd try to say a few sentences not in English and promptly give up, convinced I was babbling nonsense.

However, early one Sunday morning, I persevered. I didn't slam on the rational brakes, and this time, I began to feel that I was genuinely praying to the Lord in a new language. I felt love, joy, and genuine praise. I believed!

That afternoon, I took a service in the tiny Norfolk village of Edingthorpe. When I got there, the chapel was open but no one was around, so I went in and prayed in tongues while waiting for a congregation to turn up. Afterwards, when the service was over, the two chapel stewards, Mr and Mrs Grimes, said to me, "We knew it was going to be a lovely service this afternoon. As soon as we came into the chapel, we felt the presence of the Holy Spirit."

The very next day, a man from one of the other two churches I had visited that day phoned me from work to tell me how much the service had meant to him and his children. A lady from a different church wrote a letter to me, telling me how much more the previous Sunday's service had meant to her than the first one I took there!

I thought back to the amazing blessing that Richard Keeler had prayed over me nine months earlier. Had I started to give birth to the spiritual fruit that he had prayed I would bear? Had the Spirit's anointing on him been passed on to me?

There was no doubt that God had begun to change me. But perhaps the most extraordinary thing was that during those first aborted efforts at speaking in tongues, I had somehow got the idea that I was trying to speak in Spanish. I don't know where the idea came from because, so far as I knew, I had never heard anyone speak in Spanish. There was one word in particular that

I kept repeating.[18] Some years afterwards, when I did learn to speak Spanish, I was able to find the word in a Spanish dictionary. It meant, "Fill! Fill! Fill!" Without knowing it in my conscious mind, the Holy Spirit had been directing my prayers, pleading with the Father to fill me with his Holy Spirit. And Father God had gladly answered.

---

[18] The word 'llena'.

Chapter 9. A Miracle of Faith and Finances

I had been manning a small bookstall in the Aylsham marketplace for some months on Saturday mornings. We sold Christian greeting cards, Bibles, Bible reading notes, and associated Christian trinkets like bookmarks. It took us a lot of time to set it up and take it down, and I had the idea that if we could find a suitable small caravan it would be a lot more convenient. I arranged a church meeting at the beginning of November to discuss the idea. The members were supportive, but when I asked, "How shall we pay for it?" there was total silence. It was a bit like walking into a classroom and asking, "Who wrote 'history is boring' on the blackboard?"

In those days, Methodist ministers were paid quarterly in advance, and as November 1st was still four weeks from the end of the quarter, I had a bit of money in hand. I said, "All right. I will pay for it and I'll trust that I shall be repaid, perhaps with donations that people give me." I had total confidence that I would be repaid: there was simply no doubt in my mind. I think it must have been what is called in the Bible a 'gift of faith', and I think it's the only genuine gift of faith I have ever had.

I'd made friends with a man named Oliver Cooke, who was a member of the local Brethren church. Oliver was a second-hand car dealer, and he offered to help me find a suitable second-hand caravan. On our second visit together, we found one that was perfect: its end opened out to form a canopy, which was just what we needed. The owner wanted £85 for it. Oliver offered him £80, which he accepted. Then Oliver said,

"How about £77.50 if I give you cash?"[19] There was a slight pause, and the owner agreed.

The average weekly wage for an adult male manual worker in 1969 was £28 per week, probably similar to my stipend. Oliver paid for the caravan, and I promised to repay him with a cheque.

A local farmer offered parking space for the caravan during the week and towed it to and from the marketplace each Saturday. During the following weeks, various people gave me contributions, all of which I noted in a small red notebook. Not long before Christmas, one of the ladies in the church suggested we go out carol singing to collect more money towards it. I accepted her invitation, and we sallied forth to collect pennies and shillings for the caravan fund. Soon after Christmas, I decided to add up how much of the £77.50 I had received altogether. It came to the total amount plus a mere thirteen old pennies extra! Without making any announcement about it, I received no further donations.

I reflected that God could have given even greater proof that the money was from him if I had received the exact amount. And then the penny, or rather thirteen pennies, dropped. Having only a Trustee Savings Bank account, I'd had to pay six pence for the cheque and a further five pence for a stamp to post it to Oliver: a total of eleven pence. Amazing! But what about the other tuppence, I thought? And then I got it: the Lord had repaid me for my envelope, notepaper and ink!

A week or two later, a further, final penny dropped. I realized that out of all the people who had helped to buy the caravan, I was the only one who had contributed nothing towards it!

Recently, I've been thinking about this again. I calculated that the probability of my being paid the exact amount by chance, based on some reasonable assumptions, was perhaps

---

[19] What he actually said was seventy-seven pounds ten shillings, the equivalent of £77.50 in today's currency.

about 1 in 15,000. So I don't believe it happened by chance, especially in the light of that unusual conviction I had at the beginning that I would be fully repaid. I believe that the Lord led us to that particular caravan; that he led Oliver Cooke to offer £77.50 for it; that he prompted various people to give the amounts they gave; and that he somehow oversaw the final collection of shillings and pennies from the carol-singing to complete the exact amount required to repay me for what I had spent.

Chapter 10. New Abilities, a New Daughter and a New Destination

1970 was a particularly eventful year in our lives. It would see the birth of our daughter; the completion of my two years of ministry on probation and my ordination as a Methodist minister; an extraordinary call from God to the country where he wanted us to go; and finally, entry into a deep, dark valley confronting demonic spirits and a potentially life-changing illness.

It would also be a year in which I began to explore some of the new abilities that the Holy Spirit had given me. Jesus said, *"You shall receive power when the Holy Spirit has come upon you..."*[20] Like Saint Peter, who noticed the lame beggar sitting at one of the gates of the temple in Jerusalem, and said to him, *"In the name of Jesus Christ of Nazareth, walk,"*[21] I wanted the Spirit to do extraordinary things through me for Jesus.

So I began to take my first tentative steps of faith in the power of the Holy Spirit and in the promises of God in his Word.

Jesus said, *"My sheep hear my voice,"*[22] so I prayed with faith, asking the Lord to tell me what I should preach about on Easter Sunday. I started to write, thinking about what I was writing as little as possible, in order to allow the Lord to dictate the words. Here's just some of what I wrote:

> *In Jesus my Son, I trod down the evil one, brought deliverance and healing to everyone, and overcame death. So whatever happens, the*

---

[20] Acts 1:8
[21] Acts 3:6
[22] John 10:27

evil one is conquered, and you are now free. This means that whatever comes upon you—fear, pride, shame, hate, dishonour— there is no need to be upset because the remedy is Christ. He is your freedom, and in him you are secure.

I was encouraged that the Lord seemed to have spoken to me.

The next new thing concerned prayer in the Holy Spirit. The Bible says in Romans 8:26, '*We do not know how to pray as we ought, but the Spirit himself intercedes for us…*' When I didn't know how to pray for someone, I wanted to pray with words that the Holy Spirit gave me.

A couple in our church had a little girl whose name was Lily. She was about 18 months old. When I visited her home that April evening, I heard her crying upstairs.

"Should you go and see to Lily?" I asked her mother.

"There's no point. It's the same every night. Whatever we say or do, she'll go on crying until she's completely exhausted and then she'll go to sleep."

"Shall I try?" I asked.

Her mother gave a wry smile. "If you want to. Her bedroom is the first on the left."

I entered little Lily's bedroom, and when she saw me, she immediately stopped crying. I prayed with her and asked God to take away her fears and to give her sleep. Then I prayed quietly in tongues for her with my eyes closed. I was praying with words that the Holy Spirit gave me, because I didn't know what the problem was. I had never done this before.

When I stopped speaking and opened my eyes, Lily was fast asleep! I crept out of the bedroom, barely daring to breathe.

Lily and the rest of the family slept until 9:00 a.m. the following morning. Every night after that, she went to sleep without any problem.

❧ ❧ ❧ ❧ ❧ ❧ ❧

Next came an experience of praying for physical healing. We

had once prayed for our cat to be healed: now it was time to pray for a human being.

For several days in March, my wife hobbled around with a bout of painful sciatica. It was probably caused by our soon-to-be-born second baby sitting on a nerve. One morning, in desperation, Ann asked me to pray for her. We sat down together on the sofa. I laid my hands on her and, in the name of Jesus, I asked our Father to heal her. In Mark 16:18 Jesus said, *"These signs will accompany those who believe… They will lay their hands on the sick, and they will recover."* So that is what I did.

Ann got up, left the room, and returned half a minute later. "It's gone!" she announced. "The pain has gone."

"Did it go straight away when I prayed?" I asked.

"No, but Jesus said that God would give us what we ask him if we ask in faith, so I thought I would see if I could walk up the stairs. And halfway up, the pain left me."

This was remarkably reminiscent of ten lepers who once asked Jesus to heal them. He told them to go and show the priests that they were well, and the Bible tells us that *'As they went, they were healed.'*[23]

❧ ❧ ❧ ❧ ❧ ❧ ❧

On the last Monday in April 1970, Ann started to have contractions: our second baby was about to be born. We left home with our little boy at about 5:00 a.m., the pine trees outside our house just visible in the first light. All the birds of heaven were singing joyfully, and a light frost had turned the world silver. We drove to the maternity hospital, arriving just as the sun appeared above the horizon. In those days, husbands were not encouraged to attend a birth, so I left Ann in the care of the midwives and returned home.

In the end, our new baby changed her mind about entering the world, and I had to bring Ann home again. But she'd had a valuable rest, and the episode had helpfully shown us that

---

[23] Luke 17:14

Julian and I could survive without her, even if only for a short time. This would become important later.

The day came when our lovely Spirit-filled daughter Emerald was born. Her birth was extraordinarily special. It was nine months almost to the day after God first filled Ann with his Holy Spirit and so brought a serious postnatal depression to a sudden end; and she was born on the Day of Pentecost, 1970, when Christians celebrate the day that the Holy Spirit first fell on the Christian church. The Lord's timing was perfect. He is so clever!

%% %% %% %% %% %% %%

In July, I officially became Rev Arnold Page at an ordination service in Oldham, Greater Manchester. Three other men were ordained with me, and we were each permitted to choose a hymn to be sung during the service. There was only one choice for me: Charles Wesley's hymn, *O Thou who camest from above.*

> *Jesus, confirm my heart's desire*
> *To work, and think, and speak for Thee;*
> *Still let me guard the holy fire,*
> *And still stir up thy gift in me.*
>
> *Ready for all Thy perfect will,*
> *My acts of faith and love repeat,*
> *Till death Thy endless mercies seal,*
> *And make the sacrifice complete.*

That summer, I was asked if I would like to extend my initial three-year appointment at Aylsham by another two years after August 1971. I declined the invitation, because God's call to serve him abroad was still in our hearts. Instead, Ann and I arranged to meet someone in the Methodist Church Overseas Division towards the end of August 1970 to discuss a post overseas, which would begin twelve months later. Our calling to serve the Lord abroad would at last be fulfilled.

❧ ❧ ❧ ❧ ❧ ❧ ❧

My minister friend David and I had arranged a week's residential camp for all the young people in our churches. A Norfolk farmer in a place called Oby had converted some buildings into holiday accommodation, and he was happy to make the place available to us. Some wonderful things happened that week, but one thing in particular changed our lives. Our interviews in London being a couple of weeks away, Ann and I asked David to meet us in our caravan to pray with us and ask the Lord if there was any particular country where he wanted to send us.

As we waited on God in prayer, Ann began to see in her head a series of clear pictures—high snow-capped mountains, an inlet from the sea, a lake, people working in fields, some haystacks... David saw some of the same pictures, for at one point, he and Ann were describing the same scene together. But when he said he thought it might be Russia, my heart sank. We were still in the days of the Cold War, and any Christian missionaries in Russia would rapidly be arrested.

So I asked what the people looked like, and Ann was shown a close-up of them. She must have been seeing things so vividly! She said they were not from Africa (where I had thought we might go) nor India (which she had once thought of going to) but were more like American Indians.

And then she said, "It's South America."

"How do you know?" I asked.

"I can see a map of it," she said.

The word 'Chile' came into my mind, but I didn't say anything, in case I'd imagined it. The map zoomed in more closely.

"It's Chile!" she exclaimed.

"How do you know?" I asked again.

"I'm seeing a map of Chile. I know what the map of Chile looks like."

Now Ann saw an ancient black steam train, some native people paddling a canoe with a triangular sail, and, more worryingly, soldiers and armoured cars.

Our friend David had an unusual counselling gift. The Lord sometimes gave him the chapter and verse of the Bible to read without his necessarily knowing what it said. He'd read the verse to someone he was counselling and ask if it meant anything to them. More often than not, it did, and it would be a key to unlocking physical or mental healing or some other need. Now David said, "I think God wants us to read Isaiah chapter 49."

"You read it, and we'll listen," I said.

So David found the chapter and began reading:

Listen to me, O coastlands, and hearken, you peoples from afar. The Lord called me from the womb, from the body of my mother he named my name... And now the Lord says, "It is too light a thing that you should be my servant to raise up the tribes of Jacob and to restore the preserved of Israel; I will give you as a light to the nations, that my salvation may reach to the end of the earth."

Isaiah 49:1,6

I can't help but remark at how every verse carried such clear significance:

Listen to me, O coastlands, [Chile has a 2600-mile-long Pacific Ocean coastland] *and hearken, you peoples from afar.* [It is 7300 miles (11,700 km) from England.] *The Lord called me from the womb, from the body of my mother he named my name.* [My mother dedicated me to the Lord's service in pregnancy] *And now the Lord says, "It is too light a thing that you should be my servant to raise up the tribes of Jacob and to restore the preserved of Israel* [i.e. too easy to preach to people in your own land]*; I will give you as a light to the nations, that my salvation may reach to the end of the earth."* [Chile extends southwards to Antarctica, and Punta Arenas is the most southerly mainland city in the world.]

At this point, David said, "It is definitely a missionary call." Later, he admitted that he had not believed we should go abroad at all until that point. He read on:

> *Break forth, O mountains, into singing!* [The Andes, the second highest mountain range in the world, runs all the way down the eastern side of Chile]... *The children born in the time of your bereavement* [Isaiah was speaking about the 'bereavement' of the homeland of Israel whose children had left it—our children would be leaving England] *will yet say in your ears: "This place is too narrow for me."* [Chile is 2600 miles long and only 100 miles wide on average!]
>
> Isaiah 49:13,20

As soon as we returned home after the youth week, I went into Aylsham library to find a book about Chile. In the very first paragraph, I read, 'The name 'Chile' is thought to come from a Quecha word meaning 'Where the land ends' or '*The end of the earth*'.'! The photos in it almost exactly matched some of the scenes Ann had described!

In October that year, Chile was in the news. Chile's first Marxist president had been elected, and the streets of Santiago were filled with soldiers and armoured vehicles celebrating his victory, just as Ann had seen. Perhaps that was why David had thought it was Russia he was seeing.

Later, I learned that the most numerous and influential church denomination in Chile, apart from Roman Catholicism, was the Pentecostal Methodist Church. Probably the sole country in the world where Pentecostal Methodists constitute a defined denomination, Chile would be perfect for Ann and me. Only a real, living, loving God could be such an extraordinary matchmaker in calling us to serve him there!

Not only that, but the language spoken in Chile is Spanish, the very language that I thought I might be speaking when I first practised speaking in tongues!

When we went to London a few weeks later, we told the Methodist Church Overseas Division officials that the Lord wanted us to go to Chile. Their response was immediate. They couldn't send us to Chile because they had not received any invitation from the Chilean Methodist Church: the British Methodist Church had no relationship with the Church in Chile. They were adamant about this. Nowadays, they said, churches do not send missionaries to foreign countries without some invitation from the churches in those countries.

Despite all God's clear direction, I had no choice but to accept another appointment in England... for now.

Chapter 11. Demons, Despair and Deliverance

Ann and I were not the only people whose lives were changed that week in Oby. David noticed that one of the young people, a girl named Maisie Blackmore, seemed to be uncommonly shy and almost fearful of being addressed. He sensed that she was controlled by a spirit of fear, something Saint Paul mentioned in one of his letters.[24] I had a chat with Maisie, and offered to pray for her.

Maisie joined the three of us in our little caravan, and the instant that we began to pray she fell to the floor unconscious. This appeared to confirm David's diagnosis, so together we bound the spirit,[25] and told it to leave and never return. Maisie opened her eyes, gave a slightly bewildered little smile, and stood up. For the rest of the week she was a different person. Here's some of what she wrote to me in a letter from home a few days later.

When I settled in, I really started to enjoy myself. It was wonderful to have fellowship and fun with so many young people, but there was one thing which worried me. It was that I could not join in with the discussions, and I refused to report back on them. It was Wednesday night, I think, when we prayed in groups, and I found that I couldn't pray out loud in front of others, and this really did start me thinking. Then on Thursday afternoon I started to talk to you and then as you know we went to your caravan and the fear was taken away from me. I can't remember much about this except

---

[24] 2 Tim 1:7

[25] Jesus gave his followers power to 'bind' an evil spirit with a word of command, and advised us to do this before telling it to leave. (Matthew 18:18; Mark 3:27)

that I was very, very happy afterwards. On Friday I reported back on the discussion, I said grace at dinnertime and I prayed in the group out loud… It was so wonderful what happened to me last week that I can't stop saying "Thank you" to my Lord. I think I have grown closer to him than ever.

Later Maisie told me that on the Sunday after the camp, she asked if she could share in her church service some of the things that had happened during the youth week, and she addressed the entire adult congregation without fear.

❧ ❧ ❧ ❧ ❧ ❧ ❧

Ann had earlier driven a nasty snake-like spirit out of a woman, and now she had helped to do something similar for Maisie Blackmore. In what followed, it seemed as though a furious Satan was directing his vengeance at Ann. Three or four weeks later, after we visited London for our interviews, she started to hear voices.

Very occasionally, angels make an appearance in people's lives, and sometimes evil spirits do the same. The latter would much prefer to remain invisible, but sometimes they are goaded into revealing themselves in this visible material world, and this was one of those times. It is uncomfortable for me to share with you what happened, but I feel I must do this, because it was such a powerful demonstration of the reality of the invisible spiritual world all around us.

A travelling 'minister' had been in the area, visiting prayer groups and individuals in their homes. Unfortunately, his ministry seemed to do more harm than good, leaving some people frightened and others depressed. Though we didn't see it so clearly at the time, I now believe he was one of the false teachers Saint Paul warns about: *'men of corrupt minds and counterfeit faith who make their way into households and capture weak women…'*[26]

---

[26] 2 Timothy 3:6-8

Ann had been listening to this man, and when a voice in her head told her that she too was to be a teacher in spiritual things, the travelling 'minister' confirmed this, even though Ann told me she knew that what she had heard was not from God.

The voices said more and more ridiculous, nasty and potentially dangerous things to her—for example, that we should get together with four other people and dance around in a ring saying we loved each other; that I kept touching my nose to indicate that there was something wrong with her; and that we should make love without precautions, which could have had serious consequences due to her deteriorating mental state. On September 21st 1970, I phoned our friend David for counsel.

You are probably wondering why I didn't take my wife to consult a doctor, especially at it appeared to be another bout of post-natal mental depression. I think it was because I believed the problem was at least partly a spiritual one for which a doctor would have no remedy. And as things turned out, that was the case.

By now, David had moved away, but he travelled to visit us the next day. He prayed for Ann, and she became a little better. But that evening, all hell broke loose. Ann and I, along with Robert, a trusted young friend who had come to help minister to her, were together in our bedroom as I pleaded with the Lord to set Ann's mind free from the terrible thoughts that she was now believing. Nothing seemed to be happening, so instead, I began asking the Lord just to give her strength to survive the ordeal. My words were flooded with love, and my eyes with anguished tears.

Demons can't stand genuine love. The first demon made its presence evident.

Ann—or the demon—began to say to me, "I hate you! I hate you!" The whole shape of Ann's face, including the bone structure, changed. Her lower jaw became narrower, her teeth appeared to be sharply pointed, and her eyes looked horrible. I was not imagining these things: her appearance was literally out of this world. Ann—or the demon—rushed at me, forced me against the wardrobe door and began beating me with her fists. It was a spirit of hatred.

Robert tried to bind the spirit[27], and I told it to come out in the name of Jesus. I lifted my hands and somehow I felt the spirit lift out of her at the same moment. She collapsed on the floor at my feet, saying, "Thank you for that deliverance." That was not her usual way of speaking, and I didn't like it, but her teeth and eyes had returned to normal. The rest of her face took another half hour to recover.

The following day, it took all my strength to force open the wardrobe door again: the violence of the attack had jammed it in so tightly.

Unfortunately, that was not the end of it. During the next two days, Ann said and did things so strange and unpleasant that I'd prefer not to describe them. I phoned David again. He suggested we stay at his house, where other people he knew could help. Two families offered to look after our children while we were away.

This time, it was Jeremiah chapter 31 that God put into David's mind to read. It was so full of encouragement and comfort!

"I have loved you with an everlasting love; therefore I have continued my faithfulness to you. Again, I will build you, and you shall be built, O virgin Israel! Again, you shall adorn yourself with timbrels, and shall go forth in the dance of the merrymakers."[28]

A man in Devon whom David knew was practised in delivering people from demons. David asked him for support

---

[27] This is a reference to Jesus's words about evil spirits. *"No one can enter a strong man's house and plunder his goods, unless he first binds the strong man."* Mark 3:27 *"Truly, I say to you, whatever you bind on earth shall be bound in heaven."* Matthew 18:18

[28] Jeremiah 31:3,4

in prayer, telling him that he was going to be ministering to someone with the help of a friend, but giving no further details. David encouraged me to go to bed, while he and his friend began to pray for Ann. They were still praying at 2 a.m. when the telephone rang. It was the man from Devon.

"Hello, David. I hope I haven't woken you up."

"No, no. We are all awake."

"You asked me to pray for you. Are you ministering to someone?"

"Yes."

"Okay. Let me check. I see a lady wearing a navy blue cardigan over a pink dress. She has straight dark brown hair, and she isn't speaking. Am I right?"

"Yes, that's it."

"Good. So this is what the Lord has shown me. The lady has a religious spirit, a spirit of idolatry, and another spirit (which he named). Also, she has a split mind. She will recover from that, but it will take time."

Once David and his friend knew what the spirits were, it was easy to expel them in the name of Jesus Christ.

It had taken two—or perhaps three—people to pray into the night before the Lord intervened in this dramatic way. When they reported to me in the morning what had happened, I saw straight away that the three named spirits exactly matched Ann's words and behaviour in the preceding few days. The good news that the friend had given—such a relief—was that she would recover. Her behaviour had undoubtedly returned to normal, but she had become very withdrawn.

Knowing it would take time for Ann to recover, I asked my parents if they could look after her for a while. I didn't feel I could provide the necessary TLC as well as caring for the children and getting on with my job. However, when my parents met Ann and saw her condition they contacted a doctor, and on October 2nd it was arranged for me to take my dear wife to a major mental hospital near where they lived.

I now had a small boy and a baby girl to look after, while continuing my leadership of the churches and preaching every Sunday. With my beloved wife far away, everything was fearfully hard, but God was good. One of my sisters came to help for the first eleven days, and then my other sister came across a lady from New Zealand. This lady, Rae, had been looking for some way to serve the Lord, and she willingly came to stay with the children and me, to help with the children and the house.

The NHS had no immediate cure for Ann. The hospital was a long way from Aylsham, but I did visit her from time to time. Those visits were far from happy. Ann became totally withdrawn, not speaking, and staring blankly at me whenever I spoke to her. The Bible tells us that *'in the days of his flesh, Jesus offered up prayers and supplications with loud cries and tears.'*[29] Sometimes that was my experience too.

Ann grew thinner and thinner due to not eating, until she was a sad, pathetic shadow of what she had once been. It seemed as though she would inevitably just fade away, except for the promise I clung to. The man from Torquay had said that she would recover, but it would take time. He had been right about the other things he said, so I held onto his words as an anchor from the Lord.

The hospital staff eventually woke up Ann's brain with several sessions of ECT, which stands for electroconvulsive therapy. It involves sending an electric shock through the brain, giving the patient an epileptic fit. It must be the most barbaric treatment in the National Health Service. But somehow it worked.

Ann was discharged from hospital on February 9th, 1971, 128 days after her admission.

[Friday, February 26th 1971]

---

[29] Hebrews 5:7

I attribute my wife's survival and recovery mainly to God, who has also wonderfully kept me during all this time and has revealed more of his tender and holy love to me than I ever knew or imagined previously. He has provided Rae to look after me and the children, and through the hands of his servants, he has given me £80 towards the cost of travelling to the hospital (150 miles from here) to visit Ann every fortnight. He is a great saviour, and we shall never cease to love him. Through all that we have learnt and all that we have been made, we are better equipped and motivated to continue the fight of Jesus against the gates of hell.

Those words I wrote seem so stilted now, but I had been through an exceedingly stressful time, and their meaning is clear: I was grateful to the Lord for bringing us through 'the valley of the shadow of death'; and through the experience, I somehow felt better equipped and remotivated to serve him.

$$\text{❧ ❧ ❧ ❧ ❧ ❧ ❧}$$

God often draws nearest to us when things are at their toughest. Ann and I were due to leave Aylsham towards the end of August, but it turned out that her recent illness was not totally at an end. A month before our leaving date, she started imagining things again and became somewhat withdrawn. We consulted our GP and he arranged for her to be admitted to our local hospital. This time, I had no Rae to help me.

A couple of our age, Ced and Kath Brown, generously offered to take care of one-year-old Emerald in their own home, leaving me to care for my son. It was not easy for him or me. One night in particular, it took ages to settle him down to sleep. When I at last succeeded, I felt weak, faint and hopeless. It was all too much for me. I couldn't cope with being a father, minister and hospital visitor all at once and all on my own. I felt that I couldn't go on another day. I had finally come to the end of my resources. I said to the Lord, "O God, you've got to comfort me!"

To make things worse, the new hospital consultant had reviewed Ann's notes and he told me that this time she might never recover. So once again, I turned to the Bible for help. As Jeremiah chapter 31 had been so comforting when David had read it to us, I purposely turned to the Jeremiah book again and started to read the first words I found there. The Spirit of God led me to an astonishingly appropriate passage. I immediately felt led to interpret 'Israel and Judah' as 'Arnold and Ann' and read as follows:

> *These are the words which the Lord spoke concerning Israel and Judah: "Thus says the Lord: we have heard a cry of panic, of terror, and no peace. Ask now and see, can a man bear a child? Why then do I see every man with his hands on his loins like a woman in labour? Why has every face turned pale? Alas! That day is so great there is none like it; it is a time of distress for Jacob; yet he shall be saved out of it..."[30]*

Once more, it was as though the Lord was speaking to me directly. He knew what a distressing time I was having. He knew just how I felt. I was not alone after all. And he was telling me that Ann would recover. Never mind what the doctors thought: she would be well again!

After reading those lovely words, those oh-so-comforting words, I knew I'd be able to cope. I knew Ann would come home again and that the Lord would sustain me until she did. I read to the end of the chapter: *In the latter days, you will understand this.*[31]

The doctors in the hospital had no real idea what was wrong with my wife, but the Lord was telling me that one day we would understand, and many years later, we did.

How wonderful it is to be comforted by the Lord! The passage he found for me was without question the most

---

[30] Jeremiah 30:4-7
[31] Jeremiah 30:24

appropriate passage among all 31,102 verses in the Bible. Saint Paul describes him as '*the God of all comfort*', and he certainly proved that to be true for me.

❧ ❧ ❧ ❧ ❧ ❧ ❧

Only three weeks later, Ann was well enough to be discharged, and we left Aylsham shortly before the end of August as planned. Even if the Methodist Church had been willing to send us to Chile, Ann would not have passed the medical now, so it was as well that no arrangements had been put in motion the previous summer.

Instead, I was assigned to a new appointment, somewhere that proved to be markedly different from Norfolk.

Chapter 12. Miracles of Weather, Healing, and Two Amazing Tiny Booklets

In August 1971, we moved to the lovely little Somerset town of Castle Cary. Once voted 'Britain's Best Place to Live',[32] it felt like coming home: we were so happy there! Ann was well again, albeit on medication, and our small, modern house had only one coal fire: the rest was heated by electric storage heaters.

Several important events took place in Somerset, and we learned some lessons which significantly changed our future. But before I move on to that, I want to tell you about something that happened in Norfolk soon after we left there. While I was not directly involved, four of the main organisers were people Ann and I had introduced to the Holy Spirit, so I feel that we had some involvement, if tenuous, in the miracle that took place.

Within a few months of our leaving Aylsham, there was such a spiritual revival there that the people involved planned to hold two weeks of evangelistic meetings in the town. These were to take the form of a tent crusade the following summer, to be publicized as The North Norfolk Crusade.

Apart from the small market square, there was no public car park in Aylsham in those days, and with people travelling in from Norwich and various parts of North Norfolk, car parking was a potential problem. At last, after receiving persistent requests, the Recreation Ground committee gave permission for cars to be parked on the recreation ground, but only if the grass was dry. And that could cause a problem. If it rained on one of the crusade days, visitors would have to find somewhere to park some considerable distance from the tent, a particular

---

[32] The Muddy Stilettos Awards, September 2024.

problem for the elderly and disabled. Various prayer groups met regularly during the eight months preceding the crusade, and one topic of prayer was always the weather. The tent would be waterproof, but not the recreation ground.

The opening meeting of the crusade was scheduled for the evening of Monday, June 5th, 1972. Throughout the preceding Saturday and Sunday, it rained cats and dogs, or more accurately wild cats and wolfhounds. Parts of the recreation ground resembled a bog. On Monday morning, the day of the opening meeting, the rain continued to pour down. Jude Masters, responsible for tent security and car parking, prayed for a miracle as he had never prayed before. And the miracle came.

Starting at 2:00 p.m., a strong wind swept over Aylsham for an hour, followed by scorching hot sunshine. By 4:15 p.m., the recreation ground was as dry as a bone. It was astonishing! Cries of "Praise the Lord" were on many people's lips.

But the Lord hadn't finished yet.

The fine weather continued all that first week. On Sunday, no meetings were scheduled, so that people could attend their regular church services and the preacher could rest before the second week. And guess what happened? Yes, it rained most of Sunday. And on Monday? Once more, the weather dried up.

There was not a single evening of meetings when the weather wasn't fine and the ground wasn't dry.

❧ ❧ ❧ ❧ ❧ ❧ ❧

Not long after we arrived in Castle Cary, Lucas Greenaway, a young man in one of my new churches, had an appendicitis operation. The wound wouldn't stop bleeding, so an emergency blood donor session had to be arranged at a local factory to replenish the blood he was losing. He received blood from 300 different people, but he continued to bleed out faster than the doctors could get the blood into him. In the end, they told his parents that they couldn't save their son, and they gave him only four more hours to live.

Perhaps because they couldn't be present in the operating room, his parents returned home and prayed. The Lord gave them peace, assuring them they didn't need to worry! Simultaneously, Ann and I were praying that he would be so marvellously healed that the medical staff would have to say it was a miracle.

Two days later, Lucas was sitting up having lunch!

🌿 🌿 🌿 🌿 🌿 🌿 🌿

One of our church members asked me to arrange for his baby to be baptized. His wife answered the door.

"Yes?" she said.

"Good morning, Mrs Bennett," I replied. "I understand you'd like me to baptize your baby."

"Not really. It's my mother-in-law who wants her done."

"I see. At any rate, may I come in so that we can arrange a date?"

"All right."

I went in. She stubbed out a cigarette. I nodded in the direction of a cot.

"Is that your baby there? May I have a look at her?"

"She isn't well."

"What's wrong with her?"

"She's been sicking up her baby food, and this morning she wouldn't drink any milk either. I think I'll have to take her to the doctor's."

"May I pray for her?"

Mrs Bennett shrugged her shoulders, not so obviously as to be rude, but enough to express her feelings about it.

"If you want," she said.

So I went over to the cot and prayed. We then arranged a date for the service. Even I realized that going through the order of service in preparation for the baptism wasn't appropriate at that moment. It had hardly been a satisfactory visit.

A week later, I met Mrs Bennett in the street.

"How is your baby now?" I asked. I never was good at remembering names.

"Oh, she's okay. I did what you said when you prayed."

"What did I pray?" For the life of me, I couldn't remember. This sounded worrying.

"You prayed she would be able to keep down some milk that evening and that she would sit up next morning and have some baby food again. So I tried some milk later in the day, and that was okay, and in the evening, I gave her a little bit of food, which she took, and the next day, she was all right and sitting up like you said."

"Wonderful. I'm so glad."

"Shall I tell you something?"

"Yes, what?"

"When you came to our house, I didn't believe in God. My cousin was killed in the Aberfan disaster,[33] when all those kids were buried under a slag heap. I couldn't believe in any God after that. But when God answered your prayer, I knew that he was there. So I believe in him again now."

❧ ❧ ❧ ❧ ❧ ❧ ❧

In February 1972, I invited some 'Jesus people' from London to speak at two public meetings I arranged. A yellow double-decker bus proclaiming 'The Jesus Revolution is here!' brought eleven leather-jacketed youths to our quiet corner of Somerset, singing their theme song: 'You've got to be a baby to enter heaven.'

Although some twenty people supposedly committed their lives to Christ as a result of the Jesus people's ministry, only one or two of them grew out of spiritual babyhood and joined a church. This made me think seriously about the nature of commitment to Christ and growth in the knowledge of God.

---

[33] In 1966, a 32-metre high slag heap—spoil from a coal mine—slid down the hillside and buried Aberfan primary school in Wales, killing 28 adults and 116 children who had just started lessons for the day.

Back in Aylsham I had based my first sermon as a Methodist minister on the Bible verse *"We walk by faith, not by sight."*[34] I encouraged the congregation to believe what God has said in his Word and to act on it, whatever the world or reason or our natural senses might tell us to the contrary.

After a few months, a couple from the church came to visit me to ask me how they could know God as I appeared to. I was so embarrassed, for I didn't know how to answer them! In our training for the ministry, nobody had ever taught us, so far as I can remember, how to explain the good news of Jesus Christ and his salvation to someone in such a way that they could come to know him personally as their Saviour and Lord.

Now, after the visit of the Jesus people to Somerset, I thought things through again and I wrote two tiny booklets. They explained in simple terms, with supporting Bible verses, how to commit one's life genuinely to Jesus as both Saviour and Lord, and then how to take the essential steps for growing up in Christ through baptism in water, baptism in the Holy Spirit, prayer, Bible reading, Christian fellowship and service.

I drew some simple illustrations, and used a special small-print typewriter for the text.[35]

How to Know God told how God our creator wants us to know and love him as he knows and loves us; how he sent his son Jesus into the world to show us how we were meant to live, to encourage us to repent of our unbelief and rebellion; how he made a way through his sacrificial death and resurrection for us to receive forgiveness and the promise of everlasting life with Jesus as our saviour and king in a promised new earth to come.[36] *How to Grow with God* explained all the essential steps

---

[34] 2 Corinthians 5:7

[35] My typewriter had previously belonged to Roger Hargreaves, the author of the famous *Mr. Men* books!

[36] Hebrews 2:14; 1 John 4:19; Romans 8:29; Revelation 21:1-4.

for growing up into a true son or daughter of God like Jesus.[37] Together, they showed that Christianity is a relationship, not a religion.

With the help of the Lord and the scriptures I wrote my two little booklets, and they produced some incredible results. As a trial, I shared a copy of *How to Know God* with two teenagers who attended one of my village churches. I read it with them, and they committed their lives to Jesus. They grew in faith, one becoming a Church of England vicar, and the other an effective evangelist. They both attributed their life with Jesus to the little booklet we read together that evening.

I next took the *How to Know God* booklet to a nearby grammar school. With their teacher's blessing, I went through it with forty pupils one lunch hour. The following week, each of those who were Christians already went through the booklet with two or three of their school friends, explaining how they could receive eternal life through faith in Jesus. And some of those new believers began telling their friends in turn, as their teacher later confirmed.

Church leaders in Mere, Wiltshire, requested 200 copies of the booklet, and another 100 were ordered for use in Swindon. A girl in Wiltshire was filled with the Holy Spirit after reading *How to Grow with God*.

It's my intention to reprint both booklets and make them available on my website, https://arnoldvpage.com.

❧ ❧ ❧ ❧ ❧ ❧ ❧

[Diary, Saturday, October 7th, 1972]

Ann and I have to decide whether we will stay in this circuit for three years (until August 1974) or five years (to 1976). God gave Ann again the same pictures of Chile she had in 1970, with a few extra ones for good measure. He told us we must think carefully

---

[37] e.g. Matthew 4:4; Philippians 4:6; 1 John 1:9; Colossians 3:12–14; Acts 1:8; Mark 12:29-31; 1 Peter 2:9.

about our decision... We are wondering whether someone equipped with spiritual armour and weapons, perhaps better than we are, would be free and willing to succeed us here in 1974. If we can't find anyone suitable, we would not be happy about leaving, since it is dreadful to dig ground, plant and water crops, and then, when they are ripe, to let them rot.

Chapter 13. Adam Lockyer's Story and Two New Non-smokers

One of God's greatest miracles is how he can transform the life of someone who wants to change and genuinely trusts in him. Adam Lockyer's story is so beautiful that I have decided to include it all, even though it is longer than most of the stories in this book.

On April 2nd, 1973, we held a meeting in Castle Cary Primary School to prepare for the upcoming Mid-Somerset Crusade. I showed a film about Arthur Blessit,[38] which was watched by 120 people. Afterwards, a young man approached me.

"Excuse me," he said. "Are you anything to do with the Roman Catholic Church?"

"No," I replied. "I'm a minister in the Methodist Church here. Why do you want to know?"

"I've never been christened so I want to be christened in the Roman Catholic Church."

"Why do you want to be christened?" I asked.

"My name is Adam," he told me. "I've just got better after a nervous breakdown, and these last three weeks I can't stop thinking about God. I've listened to Trans-World Radio broadcasts and, I can't explain it, but I want to give my life to God."

"You can do that here and now," I told him.

---

[38]Arthur Blessit is an American evangelist who was 'called by Jesus to walk to every nation,' carrying a large wooden cross for publicity. By 2019 (the latest date for which I have information), he had covered 43,000 miles (69,202 km) through 324 nations. I showed the film about him because he had recently been touring Great Britain.

"Yes, but there are three problems, you see. I've never been christened, I don't know how to write, and when people argue about God, I don't know how to answer them, so I usually just walk away. That's not much use to God, is it?"

"Well, things will be different once Jesus comes into your life. The Bible says that if any man is in Christ he is a new creation, so if Jesus wants you to answer someone, he will give you the words to say."

I read him a passage from the Bible that showed[39] how God would be able to demonstrate his power to the world far better through a simple person like Adam than through a clever person. Adam was thrilled when he saw this. His eyes lit up, and he told me he longed to know the Bible like that.

"But another thing is," he said, "I don't like being different from other people. If I committed my life to God, I'd have to be different, wouldn't I?"

"Yes," I admitted. "But if becoming a Christian doesn't make you different, what's the point of becoming a Christian?"

I decided the moment had come to make use of my booklet *How to Know God*. We carefully went through it, dealing with the matters Adam had mentioned as we went. When we reached the prayer of commitment, Adam was happy for us to say it together. I then assured him that I would contact the Roman Catholic priest to see about his being 'christened', and I asked him if it would be all right for someone to visit him to help him further, to which he agreed.

After some thought and discussion, John Rendell agreed to meet Adam once a week to go through the 'Shepherding Programme' I had developed for the Mid-Somerset Crusade. John and Adam became immediate friends, and I soon heard from John the following story.

The very next day after I met Adam, one of his friends at work told him that the Bible was a lot of rubbish and that he ought to throw his Bible away. Adam, who had told me the

---

[39] 1 Corinthians 1:26-27

previous night that he could never think of anything to say, replied, "The Bible must be a better book than those novels you read, because this book has lasted for 2000 years!"

The next night, Friday the 4th of April, a friend came to my house for prayer, and together we asked the Lord to teach Adam to write. The following week, not knowing what we had prayed for him, Adam showed John how he had copied out the Bible verses in answer to the various questions in the previous week's lesson!

Another Christian friend, Ian Allingham, had to take over the shepherding programme for two weeks because John had an appointment to go into hospital. The second lesson that they went through concerned 'Doubtful Things'. After a testimony from Ian concerning this subject and a long conversation, Adam decided he should stop smoking. He hasn't smoked since, and he doesn't want to! Jesus said, *"You shall know the truth, and the truth will set you free."*[40]

Adam continued to talk to his friends about the Lord in the pub at night and at work, and they respected him for it.

When I met him for the second time, I invited him to come with me to Tilehurst Methodist Church in Reading to talk to people at the meeting about what God had done for him.

By this time, Adam had created ties with the Roman Catholic Church, having visited Father Oliver every week for baptismal preparation and having also arranged to help at St John's Priory fete on the afternoon of the Tilehurst visit. Father Oliver and the prioress weren't too happy about Adam's coming with us, but they agreed, and Adam came. It was in the car that he told us about being set free from smoking, and I told him to mention this when he spoke.

On the way, Adam told me that he was awfully nervous, which wasn't surprising, considering that he had never spoken in public before and had only just recovered from a breakdown due to extreme shyness and fear of people. But the Lord did

---

[40] John 8:32

something extraordinary, helping Adam to be entirely at ease and without fear when his time to speak came.

There were some fifty people from several Methodist churches in Reading present. They had come to hear what God had been doing in Somerset and to learn what he could do among them as well. When we all stood for some praise and worship, I struggled to find the right notes for the first unfamiliar song. Adam was standing beside me. To my surprise, I heard him singing every note correctly and without hesitation the first time through. At the end, I asked him if he had sung it before. "Never heard it in my life," he replied.

As if this were not enough, halfway through the next song, Adam put down his word sheet, from which the rest of us were singing, and continued to sing without hesitation the words of a song he had never heard before! When it had finished, we both burst out laughing and continued to laugh for the next minute or two.

Afterwards, in the car on our return journey, I remarked, "It seemed as if God put the tunes of those songs into your head." "Yes," he replied, laughing. "I gave up using the words as well in the end—I didn't need them!"

Adam gave a brief and charming talk about belief in God, which captivated his audience. In a strong Somerset accent, he spoke simply and naturally about the beauty of God's creation.

"If you find it hard to believe in God, then what I would advise you to do is to go out into the field, somewhere there are flowers, and sit down on the grass where it's quiet and have a look around you. You look at a flower and, cor!—you'll see that something lovely like a flower didn't just happen. Of course, it's easy to believe in God, like some sort of vague, mysterious force everywhere, but he is much more than that. What you should do is get very quiet and talk to him, not as a sort of mysterious power, but as a person. Talk to God as a person, and you will find him putting words into your mind that you never would have believed possible."

He told them how much the Bible meant to him now, being no longer a dry old book but really interesting.

As he was about to sit down, I reminded him about his smoking testimony, which he then gave. When he finished, I think people wanted to clap (not something one did in a church meeting, at least in those days). But there was a collective gasp when the chairwoman of the meeting told them that Adam had been a Christian for only seven weeks.

It was a great meeting. The Lord was with us, visibly breaking down suspicions and doubts in people's minds and filling us all with joy. Joy is my chief memory.

After my teaching talk, about six people met with Adam and received forgiveness and eternal life from God through faith in Jesus; seven people who wanted to receive power to be genuine witnesses to Jesus by the baptism of the Spirit met one-to-one with counsellors who gave them some initial teaching before praying for them to be filled with the Holy Spirit; and one person talked with me, when the Lord gave me the words he needed to hear. Other counselling and prayer took place as well.

All the way home (which we didn't reach until 2:00 a.m.) Adam kept asking, "When's the next one?"

In time, Adam began to lose interest in his former friends and wanted to be with other Christians. He decided he could not continue with the Catholic religion but must 'come over to our side of things'. The last I heard of him was that, having learned to read and write, he was training to become an ambulance driver.

❧ ❧ ❧ ❧ ❧ ❧ ❧

At Glastonbury Methodist Church, there was a young probationary minister named Charles Scott. Unusually for those days, Charles had a beard and smoked a pipe. When some of the people in his church were dramatically filled with the Holy Spirit, Charles wanted to find out whether what they believed was true.

He prayed that God would show him the truth about the Holy Spirit from the Bible, opened the New Testament five times at random places and wrote down the five verses he read. He showed them to me. One by one, in a systematic order, they encapsulated the Bible's teaching on baptism in the Holy Spirit! I went through the verses with him, and before long, Charles was filled with the Spirit. And, just like Adam Lockyer, on the day Charles was filled with the Spirit, he ceased to smoke a pipe.

His addiction, like all addictions, whether to tobacco, alcohol, drugs, gambling, food, excessive dieting, pornography, masturbation, self-harming or anything else, had been a cry for comfort. But Charles learned the truth of Jesus' promise[41] that he would send us another Comforter to be with us forever, the Holy Spirit, who brings us all the peace, purpose, fulfilment, self-esteem and comfort that our souls crave.

---

[41] John 14:16-17

Chapter 14. Baptism and a Third Birth

The New Testament makes it plain that when someone decides to follow Jesus, their very first step should be to get baptized. When the Bible uses the word baptize, it means total immersion, not the ceremonial sprinkling of water over babies, which most of the traditional churches call baptism.

Both Ann and I had been 'baptized' by sprinkling as babies, but for some time, Ann had wanted us both to be baptized properly. I had resisted this, not seeing it as essential. Nevertheless, whenever parents asked me to baptize their babies, I offered them a choice of either the traditional Methodist service of infant 'baptism', or a service of thanksgiving, dedication and blessing. They split 50:50 in their choice.

After a while, I observed that the dedication-and-blessing parents did at least start coming to church afterwards, whereas none of the 'baptism' parents was ever seen again with their baby. Evidently, the latter had requested the service merely out of a superstitious belief that somehow their child would be blessed by being 'baptized', even though they had no intention of bringing up their child 'in the nurture and admonition of the Lord' as they had promised to in the service.

So, at that point, I decided that (a) I would conduct no further services of infant 'baptism', and (b) I would join Ann in being baptized myself. The former decision was later to change the course of our lives.

Methodist churches don't have baptistries,[42] so we asked the pastor of an Elim Church[43] in Yeovil if he would baptize us. He

---

[42] A baptistry is a kind of small swimming pool, usually concealed under the floor in a church building, which can be opened up for use in baptismal services.

readily agreed, and our service took place on June 2nd, Whit Sunday, 1974. Beforehand, the church elders had prayerfully chosen a Bible verse for each of us—that is, they chose Bible verses for two people who were entirely unknown to them.

My verse was, *"It is the Lord who goes before you; he will be with you, he will not fail you or forsake you; do not fear or be dismayed."*[44]

The verse for Ann was, *"Call to me and I will answer you, and will tell you great and hidden things which you have not known."* It was from that man Jeremiah again![45] Ann had already received an amazing revelation concerning Chile, but there were two further occasions, which I'll tell you about later, when the Lord would help us to make life-changing decisions through words and pictures he would give to my wife.

The previous year, the Medical Committee of the Methodist Missionary Society had decided that due to Ann's history they couldn't recommend us for work anywhere overseas, now or at any time in the future. Nevertheless, Ann and I were still convinced that somehow the Lord would open a way and take us into the land he had promised, so my verse in particular was a real encouragement to hold fast to God's call to take us and our family to Chile one day. When Ann looked it up in its context in the Bible, she found that the previous verse said, *'Then Moses summoned Joshua, and said to him in the sight of all Israel, "Be strong and of good courage; for you shall go with this people into the land which the Lord has sworn to their fathers to give them!"'* What a confirmation!

After the service, a lovely Christian nurse spoke to us. She had never met us before.

"Hello," she said. "I didn't feel it was right to share this in the service, but the Lord has given me a word for you both. He

---

[43] Elim churches are a group of Christian churches which emphasise the importance of the supernatural gifts of the Holy Spirit and the promised return of Jesus Christ as king.

[44] Deuteronomy 31:8

[45] Jeremiah 33:3

has promised to reward you for your obedience; he has chosen and called you to serve him, and he will show you where you are to go."

Astonishing! In the light of all the negative talk I had received from the Methodist hierarchy, that was such an encouragement.

The Methodist Chairman of the District was the equivalent of a bishop in the Anglican Church. He disapproved strongly of what we had just done, being more concerned about maintaining the tradition of the Methodist denomination than obedience to Jesus. He was particularly concerned about my ongoing refusal to 'baptize' babies in accordance with the Methodist tradition. He even arranged for a high-ranking minister, Donald English, to meet me, in the hope of changing my mind. Donald was regarded as an 'evangelical'[46] like me, which should have ensured my respect for his arguments. He was polite and pleasant, but he inevitably failed in his mission. We are not allowed to change what the Bible says!

My appointment in Castle Cary had been due to end in another three months, at the end of August. We had told the leaders of our circuit that we would not continue there after that, as we were still convinced that somehow the Lord would open a way and take us into the land he had promised. We didn't want that to happen in the middle of another two years, leaving my churches in Somerset high and dry without a minister.

The Chairman had earlier said that because of my 'peculiar' views on baptism, he would not be able to recommend me for a further appointment, there or anywhere else. In other words, after August 31st, I would be unemployed. I don't recall being especially worried about this, and as things happened, there was no need to be. Only three days after our baptism, we learned that the Chairman had extended our appointment in Somerset

---

[46] 'Evangelical' is generally viewed as a label for people who believe what the Bible says.

by another year because he had been unable to find anyone else to replace me!

We had determined to obey the Lord, and as usual he looked after us.

The consultant at the Norfolk and Norwich Hospital had said that it would be too dangerous for Ann to have another baby, but in February 1974 she was feeling well again, so we applied to adopt a black baby instead. We were told that a decision about this would be made within two months—life was different in those days. However, by the beginning of June we had still heard nothing about this, and that was perhaps as well. For whether it was our exuberance over being baptized, or a miracle—for because of the consultant's warnings we took precautions about having another child of our own—but almost exactly nine months after we were baptized on June 2nd 1974, our third child, Joseph, was born in Yeovil Hospital on March 1st 1975. Our daughter was born precisely nine months after Ann's baptism in the Spirit, which terminated a postnatal depression, and now our second son was born nine months after our baptism in water, when it shouldn't have been possible. In a sense, neither should have been born at all!

Chapter 15. A Financial Miracle and More Lessons to be Learned

Besides baptism, the Lord had other lessons for us in Somerset. Methodist ministers were not well paid, but through my reading of the Bible, the Lord began speaking to me about tithing. In the Old Testament, the Lord told his people to give a tenth of all their produce to support the priests and the system of sacrificial worship in the temple. And he promised that if they would be faithful in doing this, he would bless them so abundantly in every material way that they would be amazed.[47] While we are not instructed explicitly in the New Testament to tithe, Jesus told us that if we want to live under his kingly rule, our righteousness must exceed that of the scribes and Pharisees. Those devout Jews rigorously obeyed the command to tithe, even down to the ridiculous practice of setting aside a tenth of the herbs they used in their cooking.

In any case, both Ann and I decided that, in obedience to the Lord, we should start giving away a tenth of all our income before tax. Choosing to do this was an enormous step of faith, for it meant believing that somehow we would still be able to feed and clothe our family on less than 90% of our disposable income and would even be blessed in doing so. On the other hand, our decision involved very little faith, because I distinctly remember saying to Ann, "If we find we can't manage, we can always stop tithing again!"

We must have started to do this during our final fourth year in Somerset. All went well for some months, but then our trust-and-obey train hit the buffers.

---

[47] Malachi 3:6-12

One morning in April 1975, as we were about to go and do the weekly shopping, I decided to check the bank balance. I had a shock. After shopping, we would be about £55 short before the end of the quarter. This was equivalent to £470 in today's (2025) currency.

One thing we had decided long before was that we would never go into debt, for the Bible says, *"Owe no man anything, except to love one another."*[48] So getting a loan to tide us over until the end of the quarter was out of the question. What were we to do? We and our children needed to eat, so we did the shopping anyway.

On returning home, there was an envelope on the doormat. I picked it up and opened it. A brief letter said, "When it was announced back in December that teachers were going to get some back pay, the Lord said to me it was something I could easily give, and you, with your plans for going to Chile, came immediately to mind. So now that it has come through, here is a cheque for £100. Maybe the Lord has already shown you a need for it. If not, I have no doubt he will soon. Praise his name!"

It was from a member of one of my churches. Accompanying the letter was a cheque for £100. In today's (2025) currency, this was worth £1500!

For the next 23 years, throughout the time we were raising our family, we continued to tithe, and we never once went into debt, even though one year I was not paid any wages.

❧ ❧ ❧ ❧ ❧ ❧ ❧

There were two further things the Lord taught me while we were in Somerset. He taught me about the creation of the world and the promised return of Jesus Christ! This isn't the place to go into detail about these important matters—I have

---

[48] Romans 13:8

done that elsewhere.[49,50] But there was something the Lord showed me that I haven't read anywhere else, and which you might find helpful.

When we ask, "Is God real?", which God are we talking about? The universally accepted statement of the Christian faith, known as the Apostles' Creed, begins with the words, "I believe in God, the Father Almighty, maker of heaven and earth…" The God revealed in the Bible, and the God in whom Jesus Christ unquestioningly believed, is the God who created heaven and earth in six literal days, and who has promised one day to create another and better earth, in which those who love him can live for ever.[51]

So did God really design and create this earth, or did the universe and life itself somehow happen by accident, with neither meaning or purpose, leaving God to make the best of how it turned out, and certainly unable to fulfil his promise to create another earth one day in the future? Which is the real God?

The main problem with believing that God created everything as the Bible says he did, is that the Bible tells us he did it only 6000 years ago, not 13.8 billion years ago, which most scientists believe is the age of the universe, and which we have all been brought up to believe. Scientific measurements clearly demonstrate that the universe is far, far older than the 6000 years taught in the first book of the Bible. There is probably nothing wrong with such measurements, except for one thing: they are based on the assumption that the universe was created naturally. And that is why they are wrong.

Suppose, just suppose, that God did make everything *supernaturally*, as the Bible tells us he did. And suppose you

---

[49] *God, Science and the Bible*. Arnold V Page, Books for Life Today, 2023.

[50] *The Date of Christ's Return*. Arnold V Page, Books for Life Today, 2022.

[51] Exodus 20:8-11; Isaiah 65:17; Revelation 21:1-5

could go back in a time machine to the seventh day when everything had just been made and was all sparklingly new. All sparklingly new and natural and real.

If you as a time traveller knew no better, you would look at Adam and almost certainly assume he was about 30 years old. If you happened to be a dentist, you might be able to prove it from his teeth. But you would be wrong, because God had made him only the day before! And the reason you would be wrong is that you would have *assumed* he had grown naturally.

If you were a wood scientist you might examine one of the trees in the Garden of Eden. You might take a core sample from the trunk, count the number of annual growth rings and conclude—scientifically and without any doubt—that it was a 100 years old. But because you *assumed* this very natural tree had grown naturally, your conclusion would be wrong.

Finally, if you were an astronomer and there had been enough room inside the time machine for the necessary instruments, you might be able to determine the distance of some of the stars. You might find one 10,000 light years away and conclude that it must be at least 10,000 years old for there to have been time for its light to reach the Earth. But if it had been made supernaturally only three days previously then even than you would be wrong. You would be wrong because you had *assumed* that it had been made naturally rather than supernaturally.

God could have made starlight shine on the earth from stars millions of light years away even before he created the stars, just as an artist can paint water falling into a pool before be paints the river to supply it, or paint a daylight scene before painting the sun. And he could have done it in any time period he chose.

Actually, even science tells us that matter and energy cannot have come into existence out of nothing *naturally*.[52] Nevertheless, most scientists begin with the assumption that the universe and life as we know it has somehow come into existence naturally. And it is only an assumption. All scientific measurements and deductions that lead to a very old age for the universe should commence with the statement, "Assuming that the universe was not created supernaturally..."

But in the Bible, God consistently tells us that he did make the universe supernaturally. He made it from nothing *by his word.*

> *By the word of the Lord the heavens were made, and all their host by the breath of his mouth. ...Let all the earth fear the Lord, let all the inhabitants of the world stand in awe of him! For he spoke, and it came to be; he commanded, and it stood forth.*
>
> Psalm 33:6,8,9

That is the God who said to me, "Tell them I'm real." That is the real God whom I know and love, a God who can do *anything*. And in the next chapter I'll give you an example.

---

[52]The First Law of Thermodynamics states that energy cannot be created or destroyed. Einstein modified this to encompass both energy and matter.

Chapter 16. A Word of Knowledge, a Miraculous Birth and a New Commission

I continued to believe that the Lord had called us to Chile—it had been such a definite, miraculous call that we couldn't believe otherwise. So after the Methodist Overseas Division people told us they could not send us to Chile, I started to teach myself Spanish and to seek another way to get there.

I applied first to the Anglican South American Missionary Society. Ann and I had interviews with them, but they said I would first have to be ordained as a Church of England clergyman, which would take several years. Furthermore, the chairman of the interview panel was unpleasantly dismissive of the idea that anyone could know the will of God with such certainty as we did. So...

I wrote to the Bishop of the Methodist Church in Chile, without receiving a reply.

I wrote to a Methodist minister whose church was in Santiago, without a reply.

I wrote to the Jotabeche Pentecostal Methodist Church of Chile in Santiago, and I did receive a reply: it was the 'wrong time'.

I wrote to the Christian and Missionary Alliance, the Gospel Mission of South America, the Regions Beyond Missionary Union, The New Tribes Mission...

I wrote to the World Council of Churches Program Unit on Justice and Service, the Intergovernmental Committee for European Migration in Geneva, the British Council, the Chilean Embassy...

In fact, between September 1974 and January 1977, I wrote to 37 different missionary and secular organizations. Some replied, and some didn't. Some said, "We do not practise what are commonly known as the 'sign gifts,'"[53] or "We are not in accord with the public or private use of sign gifts today." None of those who replied could offer an opening for us.

Despite the District Chairman's threats to refuse me any further appointments in the Methodist Church, I was appointed to lead a new group of churches at the beginning of September 1975. We were to live in the small market town of High Bentham in North Yorkshire, close to the Yorkshire Dales.

On the long car journey north, my five-year-old daughter asked, "Will there be dinosaurs in Yorkshire?"

"No, dear," I said. "No dinosaurs."

"Giraffes then?"

She looked so disappointed.

On the final lap of our migration north, we stopped off at the motorway services near Lancaster. I stood holding baby Joseph while I ate a doughnut. I turned my head to speak to Ann for a moment, and when I turned back I no longer had the doughnut. My little acquisitor was contentedly munching it, at only five months old!

We were even happier in High Bentham than we had been in Somerset. There were people in my part of the circuit, particularly young adults, who were baptized in the Spirit already, and there was much evidence of spiritual life. And the people were so friendly! Several invited us to tea, some offered to help decorate the manse, and some even offered to baby sit for us without being asked! During the first fortnight, we received several gifts of vegetables, pies, cakes and even a replacement washer for our old stone hot water bottle. We

---

[53] By 'sign gifts' I assume these organizations referred to supernatural abilities given by the Holy Sprit, such as speaking in other languages or healing the sick through a prayer of faith.

were so glad we had come to Bentham. It made us want to do all we could to help the people there.

The Bentham manse was even older than the one in Aylsham: it had been built in 1899! It had three floors, a cellar that had once been a washroom, and a coal cellar that was still in use. For once again, we were faced with coal fires to heat our home. The coalman carried our sacks of coal on his back into the back garden and tipped them down a chute into the cellar. So at least I wouldn't have to go outside in the depths of winter to bring in a bucket of coal. Progress!

I must have had a lot of energy in Bentham, because I grew a range of vegetables in the back garden, and one year, in a rare spell of hot weather, I remodelled the lawn in the front garden to make it easier to mow.

On the other side of the road from the manse, in the forecourt of the church, stood a solitary, iconic monkey-puzzle tree,[54] a species which is native to Chile. It felt as though the Lord was not letting us forget his original call to us!

So much happened during our stay in High Bentham that I could write another book about it. But this book is supposed to be about miracles of God's love, so I shall confine myself to three:

[Friday, April 23rd, 1976]

Ann and I were asked to see a girl who had been in much trouble at school the previous term. She was on insulin for diabetes, under a psychiatrist, and taking six tranquillizers a day. The girl wanted to have a Christian faith, but she couldn't seem able to accept Christ. Her psychiatrist had told her that she must stop attending Christian youth meetings (we have a weekly house meeting where between 40 and 80 young people meet for a time of worship and teaching each week) because, he said, these meetings were the cause

---

[54] Pinus araucania.

of her troubles! "I'm the only one who can heal you", he said. We told her, "He hasn't healed you yet, has he?"

As we talked to her, the Lord showed Ann a tennis racket being thrown across a court. We asked the girl about this and discovered that all her problems had begun when, in a temper, she had thrown her tennis racket at her older brother, whom she both admired and hated because he was so much more popular and able than she was.

Then the Lord revealed to Ann that three evil spirits were involved, together with their names. We prayed about them and sensed that the first two had left, but not the third, which was a spirit of anger. The girl was sitting with white clenched fists. Her face changed shape somewhat, and she could not bring herself to say "sorry" to God or her brother. We told her that saying sorry to God was the key to complete freedom, and at that, she stalked off.

However, that night, the young lady slept more soundly than she had for months. Her mother went into her bedroom several times and even shook her, thinking something must be wrong, but she couldn't wake her. In the morning, she woke up with a clear head and a tremendous sense of peace. She took no tranquillizers all day. In the evening, she went to see her doctor. He was so reassured that he decided not to prescribe any more.

Then she came to see us again. With Jesus' help, she told the Lord she had done wrong by being angry and envious and confessed her sin. We prayed again and commanded the anger spirit to leave, and all her tension left. She put her trust in Jesus to save her and she gave her life to him as Lord. Not long after, she apologised to her headmaster for her previous conduct, and he told her that she could return to school. Hallelujah!

🌿 🌿 🌿 🌿 🌿 🌿 🌿

The second miracle occurred at a Christian family camp near Carlisle. The five of us arrived at the camp on a Saturday in August, 1976. We were staying in a caravan on the campsite, and Ann was not feeling at all well. She felt and looked exhausted. It was late afternoon when the horrible cause of her fatigue revealed itself. She visited the toilet and suffered a miscarriage! It was so early in her pregnancy that we didn't yet know she was pregnant. Ann seemed to cope remarkably well with what had happened, but I had never cried so much in my whole life. I was deeply affected.

Ann was whisked off to hospital. One of the camp staff—a square-faced, serious kind of man with a square, serious way of talking—accompanied Ann to the hospital while I stayed with our three children. He prayed for Ann before handing her over to the hospital staff. They cleaned her out, and then, without consulting me, Ann asked them to permanently tie off her fallopian tubes to prevent any further pregnancies. Doubtless she couldn't face the thought of such a thing happening again. They kept her in overnight.

The next morning, someone brought Ann back to the camp.

"How are you feeling?" I asked.

"Not too bad."

"Would you like us all to go home?"

"No, not yet. I want to stay for the morning service first and see how I feel."

News of what had happened must have circulated. A lady came up to me.

"I'm so sorry to hear what happened yesterday," she said. "But now you have a member of your family in heaven."

I had never thought of that. It was such a comforting thought!

Ann and I felt sure that the tiny child had been a girl, and we named her Rebecca. I look forward to being reunited with her one day in the resurrection.

The Sunday morning service in the main tent included joyful praise, some Bible teaching, and a service of Holy Communion. At some point in the praise and worship, Ann felt something happen inside her. She was convinced that God had healed her.

So we stayed at the camp all week, which was a great blessing to all of us.

What happened next seems impossible, and unequivocally miraculous. Ann had been sterilised, and we had been advised against sexual intercourse to give her body plenty of time to recover from the miscarriage. Yet nine months less a week later, on Sunday May 1st 1977, my wife safely gave birth to our fourth child, Zachary, in Royal Lancaster Infirmary. His birth had every appearance of being full-term![55]

❧ ❧ ❧ ❧ ❧ ❧ ❧

Shortly before Christmas 1977, Bernardo Riquelme, a Pentecostal pastor in Puerto Montt in southern Chile, wrote to me. I had been in touch with him earlier, and he now invited me to join him as a leader in his church. Bernardo explained that the Chilean government accepted full-time foreign Christian missionaries provided that their sending church or missionary society paid their salary. If we could arrange that, he would like me to work with him.

I posted a copy of his letter to Pauline Webb, a lady who was responsible for the British Methodist Church's links with the Caribbean, which was as close as they got to South America. "I now have an invitation from a church in Chile," I wrote. "Can we discuss the practicalities of the Methodist Church supporting us there?"

Astonishingly, Pauline had just returned from Chile, where Juan Vasquez, the Bishop of the Chilean Methodist Church, had expressed a desire for closer links with British Methodism. After meeting me, she said she would write to ask the Bishop if he would like someone from England to work with him, preferring to explore that option before the invitation from Bernardo.

As usual, nothing much came of it, but the following summer, someone engaged a Yorkshire psychiatrist to assess

---

[55] May 1st was, of course, Labour Day!

whether Ann, in the light of her post-natal depressive illnesses, would be well enough to work abroad. Whether we arranged it or someone in the Overseas Division did, I don't recall. But I do have a copy of the psychiatrist's report. Following his extensive examination of Ann on August 4th, 1978, Dr Trevor Hollingworth concluded his report:

> *'In 1976, Mrs Page was sterilised. On examination of her mental state, I could find no evidence of any residual defect or indeed any evidence of a psychiatric illness… In conclusion, I have no hesitation in recommending the proposed trip to Chile, where she intends to do missionary work together with her husband and family. I think the chances of any recurrent depression are now virtually nil.'*

Hallelujah!!!

Later that August, Ann and I met the Methodist Church's Overseas Service Secretary, at our request, with a copy of the doctor's letter. She reluctantly agreed that we could attend formal interviews for overseas service in October, along with other missionary candidates, but was 'not hopeful' of our being sent to Chile.

In August or September, I spent a day in fasting and prayer. I wanted to know what God wanted me to do once we got to Chile. He had told us to go there, but I didn't know why. I was fairly sure it wasn't to draw stick people. Late that afternoon, in a mixture of faith and trepidation, I spoke aloud words that I trusted God's Holy Spirit would give me, just as the prophets did. The words that came out of my mouth were rather unexpected:

> *"As a master craftsman makes a key, and when it is finished, he places it in a lock, and the door opens without effort, so I have made and prepared you. And when I am ready, you will open doors that have been closed for many years, and many will enter thereby and be saved."*

Chapter 17. A 15-hour Miracle Orchestrated by the Lord

Two weeks later, I received another letter from Bernardo Riquelme, reiterating his invitation to me. So far as I knew, the Chilean Bishop had not replied to Pauline's letter, so I posted Bernardo's new letter to Pauline Webb to remind her that there was an opening for us in Puerto Montt.

The interviews in October were far more helpful and pleasant than the ones we had endured six years before. This time, the sessions were well designed, they included prayer, and they were conducted in an atmosphere of love. We were able to talk without antipathy about our call to Chile by visions and how the Lord had confirmed them to us through the Bible. We felt sure that God had been changing people's hearts in response to the prayers of many friends.

On the first of our two days of interviews, Pauline received a phone call from Juan Vasquez, the Chilean Methodist bishop. He told her he would be coming to London the following Monday before going to Spain for meetings. But first, he would be staying in England for five days. So Pauline suggested that I return to London at the end of that week to meet him, if he expressed an interest in meeting me.

Monday came and went, and the days passed by without any sign of him. It was a foretaste of life in Chile.

The Bishop eventually turned up at Mission House, entirely without notice, on the Thursday evening at about 7:00 p.m. when the building was more or less shut up for the night. Pauline was miles away, but her secretary was working late, and she heard the Bishop's quiet knock on the adjacent office door. She sat the Bishop down in Pauline's office, offered him a cup of coffee, and wondered how to contact her boss. These were the days before mobile phones.

In the meantime, Pauline was driving home along the Marylebone Road in London. Feeling tired, she said to herself, "If I see a vacant parking meter as I go by Mission House, I'll see if I can get in and make myself a cup of tea." She saw one free meter right outside the front door and parked at it. She didn't have a key to the building, and she didn't know if anyone would still be inside, but a caretaker happened to be putting out some empty milk bottles at a side door, and he let her in. On entering her office, she was astonished to find a somewhat bald and foreign-looking gentleman sitting in her chair.

"Why, Bishop Vasquez! Hello. We understood you were coming here last Monday."

The Bishop stood up and extended his hand.

"Yes, yes. But my government would not grant me a visa for more than 24 hours. I have to leave at 9:30 tomorrow morning to fly to Madrid."

"Where are you staying this evening?"

"At the Marylebone Hotel. Tell me, I know it is late, but would you be willing to take me on a little tour of London? It is my first visit here, and I would love to visit John Wesley's Chapel, especially. Please?"

Sigh… For the sake of good church relations… "Of course. I'd love to. But I must have a cup of tea first."

"No problem. Madame Pauline, when we met in Chile, I said we would like to have a closer relationship with the British Methodist Church. Methodist missionaries from the United States founded our church, but it was in England that Methodism began. If you have any suggestions…?"

Oh dear, I feel so tired. How to think of something like that at this time of night?

Her eyes alighted on a letter still on her desk. *Yes, that was it. Salvation!*

"I have a letter here from a Methodist minister who believes God wants him to work in Chile. Would you like to talk to him?" *Please say yes, please, please!*

"Sí, of course. Tonight?"

106

"No, not tonight. He lives in Yorkshire. It would have to be tomorrow morning before you leave your hotel."

And so it was that around 8 o'clock that Thursday evening, when I was at a church meeting in Ingleton, a telephone message came to me via my wife, asking me to travel down on the night train to meet Pauline at Euston station in London for a breakfast meeting with the Bishop of the Methodist Church in Chile!

I reached Euston station at 2:12 am. Pauline met me, and I spent the rest of the night at her flat. After an early breakfast, we drove to the hotel. There was—naturally—one vacant parking meter outside the main entrance, with 1¼ hours' prepaid parking on it.

The Bishop told me that his church had agreed to take responsibility for some fifty troublesome teenagers who were to be housed in Puerto Montt. The plan was that a 23-year-old minister who was about to be married would be appointed pastor of the Methodist Church in that city; that a Chilean couple would live in the new village itself to supervise the 'children'; and that I would assist in the church and act as a spiritual pastor to the teenagers, offering them some practical training from my engineering experience. He said we could start in September 1979, going first to a three-month language training school run by the church in the capital and **then** going south to begin work in February, when the Chilean church year started.

In prayer times earlier that year, the Lord had indeed shown us a white building in Santiago, and that we would go there first, and afterwards go south. Furthermore, towards the end of our time in Bentham, I had become mentally and emotionally burnt out. Sermon-writing, choosing hymns, and the endless round of administrative meetings meant that my heart was no longer fully engaged in ministry. I was even struggling again with my ancient enemy: getting out of bed in the morning. I passionately hoped that whatever I was to do in Chile would not be running a church full-time. So the Bishop's plan seemed perfect. I accepted his invitation.

He promised to write the proposal in more detail in English and submit it to the Overseas Division for their approval, in the hope of completing the arrangements by the end of the year.

If Bernardo Riquelme hadn't written to me when he did; if Pauline hadn't left his letter on her desk to remind her; if the Bishop hadn't stopped off in London before going to Madrid; if Pauline hadn't been been driving past Mission House on her way home that evening; if there hadn't been a free parking meter outside the main entrance; if the caretaker hadn't been putting out the milk at that moment to let her in; if Pauline hadn't felt tired and had simply driven past…!

At some point in 1979, we were told that an agreement between the British and Chilean Methodist Churches had been reached. We were to leave High Bentham at the end of August and stay in a house in Bristol while final arrangements were made for us to travel to Chile later in the autumn. I hired a Luton box van and drove across the Pennines to Harrogate, where the Yorkshire Tea Company carried out their business. Assuming we would move to Chile permanently, I bought forty tea chests for 50p each to carry all our belongings by sea to our new home. My wonderful wife Ann packed one tea chest daily until we left Bentham. She made a list of the contents for each chest, numbering each one.

In the end, we had to spend almost three months waiting in Bristol, but this gave me all the time I needed to recover from my earlier burnout and an opportunity to read and to enjoy worshipping God at a brilliant Pentecostal church which met at the top of Whiteladies Road.[56] Our children were able to go to school locally.

Finally, one frosty November day in 1979[57], a yellow rented estate car carried six people and their suitcases to Gatwick

---

[56] The Mount of Olives Assemblies of God church.

[57] November 20th, 1979

Airport in readiness for their 22-hour flight to Chile. My mother came to the airport to see us off.

Only a week before we left England, my proposed work in Chile had been changed. Bishop Vasquez telephoned Mission House to say that the money to fund the project in Puerto Montt, which a developmental organisation in Germany had promised, had not been forthcoming after all. So instead, I was to be stationed with an experienced Anglican presbyter in the city of Punta Arenas, where there was an Anglican community who spoke English and a bi-lingual Anglican school. The Methodist Church in Chile would pay me and provide a house for us. It sounded perfect, if not for me, at least for the rest of my family.

Of course, being Chile, it never happened. Well, barely any of it.

Chapter 18. At the End of the Earth

It was a heart-stopping moment. Looking out from the beautiful blue, white, and gold British Caledonian aircraft that had brought us all the way from England, we could see below us the Andes mountains—the jagged, majestic, snow-capped peaks that God had shown Ann so clearly nine years earlier. Yes, beneath us was the land that God had promised would be our new home: the land where, as a key fashioned by his hand, I was destined to unlock unimagined doors.

Marcio Sewell, who had been liaising with Mission House during the previous fortnight, met us at the airport in Santiago. As he drove us in his orange pickup truck to where we were to stay, we seemed to be travelling through a bombsite: derelict plots of land, buildings falling to pieces, newer ones only half-built. So this was what South America was like!

We drove by the headquarters of the largest church in Chile, the Jotabeche 'Evangelical Cathedral'. The building occupies an entire block in Santiago's main street, Bernardo O'Higgins Avenue.[58] It seats 15,000 people, but the church's total membership in Santiago was huge, with 350,000 regular attendees meeting in 250 locations around the city. At that time, the senior pastor, Javier Vásquez Valencia, conducted 380 marriages and more than 2,000 baptisms every year.[59] "The people believe in the power of the Holy Spirit, but in addition, every member is an evangelist," he said in an interview with a national daily paper in 1980. "The factory worker, the domestic

---

[58] Bernardo O'Higgins was half-Irish, and somehow, he became the successful leader of Chile's war of independence from Spain.

[59] The following year, I attended a weeknight service there when 35 mothers queued up to have their babies baptized. Yes, the Church practises infant baptism! Like most Pentecostal churches in Chile, its origin was in Methodism.

employee, and the student talk about their faith to their fellows and friends, invite them to our services, and when they come for the first time, they are surprised to discover a simple church without images, and simple people who believe what they say and preach, and they are converted to the Gospel... Street preachers have to spread the Gospel, but before going out to preach, they have classes to learn how to do it."

Marcio explained that we would initially stay at the Methodist Institute of Training and Service while proper accommodation was found for us.

❧ ❧ ❧ ❧ ❧ ❧ ❧

The sun was preparing for its nightly rest as our family's longest-ever day finally drew to its close. The children were asleep in bed, and Ann was getting ready, too. I went into the yard. It was quiet and peaceful outside. The air was still warm, for summer had begun, but less than fifty miles to the east, crumpled sheets of snow still shrouded the high horizon of the Andes Mountains.

I waited with my camera for the setting sun to clear the low branch of a yellow jacaranda tree and pose for me before it retired for the night beneath the western hills. I waited for it to move, as usual, a little to the right, and I waited, until I realized it wasn't moving to the right, but to the left! *"How can that be?"* I asked myself. *"The earth is still turning in the same direction as it does in England. So why...?"* It took me a moment or two to realize that the sun was still travelling from east to west, but in the southern hemisphere, everything was upside down.

The present, as well as the past, was now a foreign country. And the future country? Would it be more foreign than anything I had imagined...?

Beyond the jacaranda tree, the hazy hills kissed the sun goodnight.

❧ ❧ ❧ ❧ ❧ ❧ ❧

Each afternoon, Julian and Emerald had a Spanish lesson, while

I had three lessons a week with a resident Methodist minister. Of the promised three-month language training school there was no sign. I had spent years teaching myself Spanish, but I couldn't understand a single word that anybody said! They could understand me, but I couldn't understand them, because I had never heard the language spoken. So I had to ask them to speak very slowly; and even then it wasn't easy to begin with.

Our two youngest children attended a nursery school. Joseph was in the 'little deers' and Zachary in the 'chickens'. The young schoolchildren sang the Chilean national anthem at the end of morning assembly each day. I have never heard anyone sing their country's national anthem with such enthusiasm. They had no doubt that Chile was the best country in the world!

Our first impressions of Santiago while driving from the airport had been misleading. The city centre was largely clean, the buildings were generally in good repair, and so far as I recall, there was little graffiti or rubbish in the streets. I loved the Plaza de Armas, the central square, which was the heart of the city. When we were there, it was filled with artists painting colourful pictures for sale to tourists and collectors. Facing the square was the Metropolitan Cathedral, the main Post Office (what we would call a listed building), and the principal government building, the Palacio de la Moneda, which the Chilean Air Force had deliberately bombed in a military take-over from the Marxist president, Salvador Allende.

One day, a lady from the Institute took us all to San Cristóbal Hill, the site of the Chilean National Zoo and some beautiful gardens. A funicular railway took us to the summit, where there was a 22-metre-high statue of the Virgin Mary.

One day, I got chatting to a street shoe-shiner named Luis. We were soon surrounded by three or four street urchins—the most appropriate word to describe them—intrigued to meet someone from England. In London, I would never stop to chat with a street vendor. Somehow, in Chile, I was different.

The people in the Institute were kind, but our stay in Santiago was the closest thing to hell we had ever experienced. For two weeks, all six of us lived in one room at the Centre. After the frosty weather in Britain, the heat was insufferable: it drained all our energy. For several days, we could do little more than lie on our beds. One day, I managed to go for a walk with our children. I was so weak I had to keep sitting down on the pavement. Next, we all contracted gastric enteritis, and for a couple of days we were racing each other to the toilet. Americans prefer to call it a rest room, but it didn't get much rest from us.

After two weeks, they found us a house to live in. It was a beautiful, single-storey house not far from the Institute. A grapevine grew in an enclosed courtyard, and there was separate accommodation for a maid, so there was plenty of room for us all. Unhappily, we soon discovered that we were not the house's only inhabitants: it was infested with fleas. The children couldn't sleep at night, and my legs were bitten so severely that the scars lasted for months. Does 'love your enemies' include fleas? Joseph became adept at catching them one at a time in a bottle.

After three weeks of this purgatory, we returned to our single room in the Institute, only to find that we had brought some of the fleas with us!

Another extremely upsetting thing was that the forty tea chests of our belongings shipped from England had not turned up in the port. Again and again, I tried to get some information about them from the Bishop, but he was never available. Furthermore, I had forgotten that we were destined to go to Punta Arenas, so I didn't know where we were supposed to go or what we were supposed to be doing, and nobody I spoke to knew either.

Our family's Christmas dinner that year consisted of some substandard beef burgers at an otherwise deserted fast food restaurant. I thought it would be a special treat for the children...

In the restaurant, in every shop, and even on the metro, it seemed that all we heard, endlessly repeated, were the Buggles singing, *Video killed the radio star*. There's a line in that song, "We can't rewind, we've gone too far." I can honestly say that if we had not been so certain that coming to Chile was God's will, I would have telephoned Mission House in London and asked them to take us all back to England.

※ ※ ※ ※ ※ ※ ※

On December 30th, I was told we would be flying to Punta Arenas the following day, since no suitable ships to take us south had been found. Most people in Santiago had never been so far south: it was 1300 miles away, in the Chilean region of Antarctica. Someone told me how, in the winter, the airport would be snowed up for two or three weeks on end, preventing supplies from coming through, and that all the cars had to have special heaters in them so that their engines would start in the sub-zero temperatures.

As we said goodbye to our friends in the Centre, one elderly pastor shook Ann's hand and said, in Spanish of course, "Goodbye, my dear. You are a very brave woman." I could swear she turned pale.

※ ※ ※ ※ ※ ※ ※

After a three-hour flight, our plane touched down at the city's Presidente Carlos Ibáñez international airport. I think it was about four o'clock in the afternoon. The aircraft taxied off the runway and came to a halt. The cabin doors opened, and we climbed down the air stairs onto the apron. The temperature was pleasant, and the ground was wet with rain: through cracks, some daisies and dandelions were growing. Yes, daisies and dandelions, just like in England. I could hardly believe it. I felt as though we had come home!

A stocky man wearing a beanie, with a smiley, homely-looking woman at his side, greeted us in the terminal. In passably good English, the man introduced himself as Pastor

José Pulgar and his wife as Carris. "Welcome to Punta Arenas," they said. The people in Santiago had given them less than 24 hours' notice that we were coming.

It turned out that I was not to assist an 'experienced Anglican presbyter', as Marcio Sewell had informed Mission House in London: there was no such person in the entire city. Instead, I was to work with this friendly Methodist pastor. And that was not all that had changed. We had been told that the Chilean Church would provide accommodation for us, but they never did: we would have to rent our own house.

So, for our first two weeks in Punta Arenas, we all had to share one bedroom again, this time in the Pulgars' house. It was an incredible sacrifice for them because they had four children of their own, although two of them were living elsewhere. Where all the beds came from, I do not know. José and Carris must have slept on sofas in the living room.

Somehow, Carris cooked for ten people every day. It must have cost her a fortune in time and money. One day, I commented that the food was much the same as the food we ate in England. Carris said that wasn't surprising: her mother had taught her to cook, and her mother was Welsh! José and Carris were heroes.

Because we arrived on New Year's Eve, there was a Watch Night service at the Central Methodist Church. We all attended it, and it was lovely to sing chorus-like songs again after the more formal hymns in Santiago, especially as we already knew one of them in Spanish.

Members of the congregation stood at the communion rail, praying aloud for the work of God as the New Year began, heralded by honking car horns in the streets and hooting ships' horns in the port. Half an hour later, we joined the Pulgars and their family in their back yard for a barbecue. José roasted half a lamb that someone had given him. Our children thought it was marvellous. What a way to start a new year!

The following afternoon, I went for an exploratory walk on my own. The streets were empty—perhaps people were still recovering from the previous night's celebrations. I headed to the docks. On the way, I had a tremendous sense of safety. It wasn't that I had felt unsafe in Santiago, but here in Punta Arenas it was different. I felt utterly secure. I have never had that same feeling anywhere else or since.

When we first told my parents that we were going to live in Chile during the presidency of the military dictator Augusto Pinochet, my mother was dreadfully concerned. "Will you all be safe there?" she asked. Ann replied, "There is no safer place on earth than where God wants us to be."

In the city, buildings of all shapes, sizes and colours jostled for space next to each other, like children's coloured wooden bricks tipped out onto the carpet. A massive statue of Ferdinand Magellan standing astride a ship's cannon dominated the main square. Among the other figures around the statue's base was one of the region's now-extinct native inhabitants, whose footprints led to the belief that they had large feet. The man had a large big toe, and I later learned the folklore that if you kiss it, you will return to the city. I did, and I did!

Our tea chests arrived at last. I was sad, because a metal toolbox I had made during my apprenticeship days and the tools inside it, including several I had made, had been stolen. The insurers recompensed me, but the items themselves could never be replaced. But at least the rest of our possessions were with us once more. For nine or ten weeks, we had been living out of the suitcases we had brought with us on the aircraft.

It turned out that the dire warnings we had listened to in Santiago were totally unfounded. The climate in Punta Arenas was similar to that of Newcastle in England. And the Lord wonderfully confirmed that we were precisely where he wanted us to be. José told us that his church had hosted a nationwide conference for Methodist women two years earlier. The organizers had erected a banner across the entrance, which said, in Spanish, 'Welcome to the End of the Earth!'

Chapter 19. A Miraculous Journey and Preparations for a Crusade

We had been informed that there was a British School in the city, and this was true, but only the reception class was taught in English. A week before the school year began in March, the only other teacher of English unexpectedly resigned, so Ann, as a qualified teacher, was immediately able to replace her. She taught English to the older classes, knowing only three phrases in Spanish: "Sit down! Stop talking! Shut up!"

The income from Ann's teaching was sufficient to pay for our rent.

Emerald in particular soon picked up Spanish. At the end of the school year, she was awarded a joint first-in-class prize. This was presented at the 'Anal' Prize-giving, when the school choir enthusiastically sang *The Call of the Buggle*! (sic)

※ ※ ※ ※ ※ ※ ※

By October 1980, it had become clear that our oldest son was not coping with life in a foreign country. My sister Geraldine and her husband had generously offered Julian a home in England if he found life difficult in Chile, but it was hard to know whether he would be even less happy living apart from his own family. Ann and I were praying about this difficult choice one Monday evening, when the Lord told Ann that we should take up my sister's offer. We talked to Julian about it, and he agreed. So the plan was for Ann to take him back to the UK.

We were in the process of applying for permanent residence in Chile, and because of the situation with our passports, the trip would either have to be that same week, or six months later, after our passports had been processed in Santiago. Clearly, it had to be that week.

The next day, I visited a travel agent to book a return ticket for Ann and a single ticket for Julian for a flight to England on the Saturday.

"That will cost £1,180 in total, sir," said the travel agent lady, but in Spanish and in pesos. "Will you pay in full or by credit?"

"I would like to pay in full…" I replied, trying to work out how to say tactfully in Spanish, "but I don't have that kind of money."

Before I could finish, she continued. "Very good, sir. If you return on Thursday, I'll have the tickets ready. You can pay for them then."

I thought, *"The Lord is in this; I'll go with the flow."* I went home and told Ann what had happened.

"What do you think we should do?" I asked her.

"Why don't you go to the post office tomorrow and see if there is something in the post for us?" she suggested.

So on Wednesday I returned to the city centre and opened our mailbox in the post office. Sure enough, there was a letter for me from London. The Overseas Division had decided to reimburse us for eight months of the rent that we had paid! They said they had written to the Bishop, demanding that henceforth the Chilean Church must pay for our accommodation as they had agreed to do. (They never did.)

Enclosed with their letter was a cheque for £1,200. It was precisely enough to pay for the air tickets at £1,180 and a taxi from the airport to my sister's house in England. (In 1981, the extra £20 was worth £96 today, 2025.) Once in England, Ann would be able to draw out money from our English bank account for her needs in England and any expenses on the return trip. I took the cheque into our bank, where they knew me by then, and exchanged it for cash.

Why eight months' rent, when we had paid for over nine months to that date? And why did it come on that particular day, the day I needed it? Once again, the Lord had provided the exact amount we needed at the exact time. He is such a great accountant!

The next day, I returned to the travel agent and paid the full price of the tickets. So far as I was concerned, they had cost us nothing.

Incidentally, do you remember how I told you about the two teenagers with whom I shared my *How to Know God* booklet for the first time and how one of them later became a Church of England vicar? Well, in 1980, the young lady concerned had not yet embarked on her ecclesiastical career, but the Lord told her in a dream that she was to come to Chile, a commission that was independently confirmed by a word of knowledge[60] from a friend of hers. And somehow, while my wife was in England with Julian, she and Charlotte got in touch with each other, and they came back to Chile together!

How they both worked what followed I never found out, but the British Trade Attaché met them at the airport in Santiago and fast-tracked them through customs before inviting them to spend the night with himself and his wife in their luxurious Santiago residence, before they flew south to Punta Arenas!

Charlotte could speak Spanish, so she too got a job as a teacher at the British School. Not only that, she took on responsibility for some English-speaking services at St James's Church next door, where there was no resident vicar.

Because our son was no longer living with us, Charlotte was able to have his bedroom and live with us until a family from our church built a little house for her in their back garden. Who but God could have timed and arranged all that so well?

---

[60] A 'word of knowledge' is a useful fact that the Holy Spirit reveals to someone. In this case the Lord evidently wanted Charlotte to serve him in Chile.

✿ ✿ ✿ ✿ ✿ ✿ ✿

People who like to have everything planned and to know in advance what is going to happen would find it hard to live in Chile. It was not unusual for me to prepare a Sunday School lesson for children and then be asked, on arrival at the church, to take the adult class instead, as the adult teacher hadn't turned up. My resulting teaching would inevitably be somewhat rough and ready, but the people would invariably express their appreciation.

If we arranged to do something at a particular time, I would often be asked, "Is that Chilean time or English time?" I always replied, "English time," but as often as not the arrangement would revert to Chilean time, and whatever it was would start half an hour or an hour later than planned, if it started it all!

Every Sunday afternoon, I walked a mile to the third of the three Methodist chapels in the city. It was in a poor neighbourhood, Población Dieciocho (Community Eighteen). A queue of some fifteen children would greet me outside the chapel, waiting for me to let them in, but only after every one of them had given me a wet kiss. They were so sweet! What I taught them without any published lesson material I do not know. I don't think I could do that now. As I wrote earlier, I was different in Chile.

✿ ✿ ✿ ✿ ✿ ✿ ✿

I was in my office in the Central Methodist Church, about to begin my daily Bible reading. All at once, some words came into my head, as plainly as if I'd heard them aloud:

"I am going to speak to you, but first, I want you to pray that you will understand what I say."

What was this about? It was strange but exciting. I did as I was told:

"Lord God, please help me to understand what you are going to say."

I waited. Nothing. The line had gone dead.

I decided to read the passage set for that day in my Bible-reading notes. It was a story Jesus told about a man who had no food in his house for an unexpected guest. Although it was late at night, the man cheekily knocked on his neighbour's door to ask him for some bread. I tried to imagine the scene…

Knock. Knock.

"Who's there? What do you want?"

"It's me, Zak. Can you let me have a loaf of bread?"

"What? No, I can't. We're all in bed. Go away. Come back in the morning if you must."

"I can't. I've got a visitor and nothing to give him. I can't send him to bed hungry."

(Hospitality was a big thing in those days.)

"That's your fault. Stop knocking and go away. You'll wake the kids up. I'm not getting out of bed for you, do you understand?"

KNOCK, KNOCK.

"Oh, for goodness' sake! All right, I'll give you what you're asking for."

I scratched my head. Was God trying to say something to me through this?

🌿 🌿 🌿 🌿 🌿 🌿 🌿

When we lived in Somerset, I had attended a small tent mission run by a young evangelist named Don Double.

Don's ministry grew, and while we were living in Bentham I invited him and his team to lead an evangelistic mission in conjunction with one of my churches there. This gave me experience in organizing an evangelistic mission, and in caring for the people who would decide to follow Christ as a result.

We had kept in touch, and one day in Punta Arenas, I received a letter from Don. He and his associate Mike Darwood were going to be in Santiago, and he asked me if I would like to meet them there. I showed the letter to José.

"Why don't you ask them to come here instead," José suggested. "Foreign missionaries never come down here."

Don agreed to come and preach, but on several conditions: that I organize and publicize public meetings involving as many churches as possible; provide a venue, stewards and at least one competent interpreter; and train counsellors to follow up people who made a decision for Christ.

I set to work recruiting the leaders of as many evangelical churches in the city as possible to help them prepare for a major four-day interdenominational event in which their members could participate. Ministers from eleven churches committed themselves to pray, plan, and support the Good News Crusade evangelists, making this the city's most influential and united crusade ever known.

I wrote some advice for counsellors and gave copies to the pastors to help them prepare some of their members for this work. The role of a counsellor was to talk to people who decided at the meetings to follow Jesus, to help them to repent of past unbelief and disobedience, to commit their lives to follow Jesus as Lord and Saviour and to integrate with a local church.

As anyone who has tried to organise church events would recognise, it was miraculous how easily everything came together. Surely I had unlocked a door through which people were gathering from many different directions. We swiftly obtained two excellent interpreters, both from hundreds of miles away: Ian Morrison, a bilingual bishop of the Anglican Church came from Chile's second biggest city Concepción; and Roger Cunningham, an American missionary and Chilean Methodist Minister flew down from Santiago.

A singer-evangelist named Carlos Pinol turned up unexpectedly at the Assemblies of God church. The combined choirs of two Baptist churches practised various songs, including a special crusade theme song, 'Christ is the only hope'. The Salvation Army captain took on overall responsibility for training the counsellors, and someone else recruited a team of stewards.

Somebody—I've no idea who—publicized the event and venue at the shortest of notice, so effectively that hundreds of people came to the meetings, including all the civic leaders. And all this without social media to help!

There was only one thing missing, and it was rather important: we needed somewhere to meet! Most of the church buildings were too small for the numbers we anticipated, and in any case, we wanted a public venue that non-churchgoers would feel comfortable entering. I had tried two sports halls, a small theatre off the main square, and even the Municipal Theatre, but everywhere I tried was booked for other events. So we found ourselves with a severe problem: Don's visit was only a fortnight away, and we had no venue!

Back in my office I was still scratching my head over Jesus's story in the Bible. Was there something I had already asked for without success, something the Lord wanted me to ask for again? What could it be? And then the penny, or rather the peso, dropped. Of course! That must be what God meant! We were to ask again for one of the venues where I'd previously been refused.

I went to speak to José and told him what I believed the Lord was telling us to do. José was such a great man. He accepted what I said without raising an eyebrow.

"Which venue do you suggest?" he asked me.

"The Municipal Theatre is best. It's central, has car parking, and comfortable seats. Let's try that."

"All right. I think the mayor might be the person to speak to," José told me.

"Will you speak to him, please? Your Spanish is better than mine. Tell him we need it for four evenings, Thursday to Sunday."

There was no way I was going to try in Spanish to persuade a Roman Catholic mayor, who probably wouldn't even approve of our evangelizing his citizens, to change his mind.

José returned from the telephone.

"I spoke to the mayor. He asked me what we wanted the theatre for, and then he looked in the diary. He said the theatre is booked for the Thursday and Friday evenings, but no shows are booked for Saturday and Sunday, so we can have it for those two evenings at least. What's more, he says we can have it free of charge as his contribution to the crusade!"

In the end, we held the first two meetings in the Methodist Church, which was quite big enough, and the two principal weekend meetings in the theatre, which was nearly full.

I don't know how God worked it all out, but I knew that he had definitely spoken to me. I couldn't help but think back to all those years ago when I wanted him to speak to me and he didn't seem to do it, and now he was!

Chapter 20. Conversions, Healings, Spirit Baptisms and More.

On the Saturday evening, all the regional heads of General Pinochet's army, navy, air force and military police attended the meeting in the Municipal Theatre along with their wives, the head of the university and the mayor, the man who had made the theatre available to us. They filled the front row of the theatre. The military men were in their uniforms, medals and all; the mayor wore his chain of office; and the ladies in glamorous dresses looked stunningly beautiful.

One reason for the attendance of all these important people was, no doubt, the novelty of meeting two English evangelists, but I think another reason was to celebrate publicly the news that the Pope had declared in favour of Chile in a dispute with Argentina about three tiny Chilean islands near Cape Horn that the Argentines claimed were theirs. The meeting began with heartfelt prayers of thanks to God for being on Chile's side.

The united Baptist choirs led such joyful praise that even the glamorous ladies in the front row clapped in time with the music.

Don's preaching and Mike's teaching always included the news that Jesus can heal the sick in the body as well as the sin-sick soul. So at one point, Don invited people who had given their lives to Christ on one of the preceding two evenings or who had been physically healed through faith in Jesus to step onto the stage and tell the rest of us what had happened.

One of the first to speak was a man from our church.

"I've been the president of the church council at the Central Methodist Church for twenty years, and I fully believed that I was a Christian," he said. "But this week, Don has taught me that we have to be born again by faith in Jesus: only Jesus can put us right with God, and he has done that for me. I have asked Jesus to be my Saviour and Lord, and I know now that my life will never be the same again."

74-year-old Emiliano Kusanovic had emigrated from Croatia many years earlier, and he had attended the meeting at our church the previous evening. Two family members had helped him to a seat because it was so difficult for him to walk, following a fall from an upper window he'd been cleaning eight months earlier. He had been sitting right in front of me in the church when Mike asked him if he wanted to be healed.

"I said, yes, of course I want to be healed," Emiliano told the theatre audience. "Then Mr Darwood asked if I believed that Jesus could heal me. And I told him 'Yes'. Then he said, 'Do you believe that Jesus will heal you now?' 'Yes,' I said, 'I do.'

"He asked Jesus to heal my legs so I could walk again. And nothing happened. I went home the same as I came. But listen! When I woke up this morning, I started to get out of bed very cautiously as usual, because it always hurt so much when I stood up. But today, it didn't hurt. It didn't hurt at all! And now I am going to show you something."

Unaided, Emiliano proceeded to march like a soldier from one side of the stage to the other and back again. "I challenge anyone in this theatre to walk better than I can!" he shouted. The audience erupted!

Following the crusade, Emiliano spent many days walking the streets around his home, testifying to everyone he met about the Lord's saving power.

That night, after some teaching from Mike and a simple but powerful message from Don, many people accepted Christ as their Saviour and Lord. The mayor's wife was believed to be one of them.

Don then invited everyone who needed physical healing to stand in the aisles for prayer. I can't remember whether there were two or four aisles, but I do remember that people were queuing for almost their entire length. Ann and I stood at the head of one queue, praying for people in turn, while the two interpreters and perhaps two of the pastors were in the other queue or queues doing the same thing.

Among the people Ann and I prayed for was a young lady named Valeria Zuñiga. She was completely deaf in one ear, and the Lord healed it. Until then, Hector, her father, had had no time for God, but this beautiful surprise encouraged him and his wife to pray for their daughter themselves a week later. This time, they asked God to restore one of her legs, which was five centimetres shorter than the other, and the Lord granted their request. Hector was so excited that the following Sunday he turned up in our Central Methodist Church to thank God publicly, which he did by standing in the pulpit and playing a hymn of praise on his mouth organ!

Joseph's schoolteacher, Margaret Harper, received prayer for her right arm, which she couldn't raise. There was no immediate improvement, but the following evening she accepted Jesus as her Saviour and asked him to fill her with the Holy Spirit. Those who wanted to be filled with the Spirit were asked to raise their hands in worship, and she suddenly found she could raise both hands high in the air without difficulty. The next moment, she was praising the Lord in a new language given to her by the Spirit!

That Sunday evening, Ann herself asked for prayer about her back, and the Lord straightened it! She was visibly taller afterwards and was able to make all the beds back home without having to rest afterwards, as she usually did. She didn't even feel tired.

Altogether, there were four evangelistic meetings, three teaching meetings (two for all Christians and one for pastors and leaders), and two special Sunday services. There was even an evangelistic meeting in the illustrious British Club.[61]

---

[61] This club had been founded in 1899 exclusively for English-speaking upper-class gentlemen, providing them with a bar, billiard tables and other gentlemanly pastimes. There were photographs on the wall of the

On Monday afternoon, the mayor telephoned José Pulgar. He thanked us for the evangelists' visit and said that he had never felt God's presence so real as he had on Saturday evening in the Municipal Theatre.

Over the four days of the crusade, about 100 people decided to follow Jesus. About three-quarters of these accepted Jesus as their Saviour and Lord for the first time. Many people received physical healing, and on the Sunday night, over 100 people sought the baptism of the Holy Spirit or to be filled anew with his power.

After they all went home, the Lord continued to heal people, and church members began to pray for each other. José believed that the Lord had removed stones from his kidneys because all the previous pain had disappeared. The following Sunday night, many people in our church recommitted themselves to the Lord's service. The service in one of the Baptist churches lasted three and a half hours! One Saturday soon afterwards, the young people in our church preached in the main square of the city for the first time, using songs and drama as well as the spoken word. As a result, many other young people attended the evening service the next day.

[News and Prayer Letter no. 5, December 1980]

In our church, we have 52 new Christians to care for. Each week, I meet 26 'guides', members of our church who will visit each new Christian once a week for the next three months, following instructions and a course of Bible study I wrote. I am like a shepherd, the 'guides' are the sheep, and the new Christians are their little lambs. The lambs have twenty-one simple Bible studies to

---

Imperial Trans-Antarctic Expedition of 1914-16, led by Sir Ernest Shackleton, who had made it a base for his operations in the South Atlantic Sea. However, by the time we lived in Punta Arenas most of its patrons were old ladies. Our meeting in the club was possibly the last public meeting ever held there, for it finally closed the following year.

do, and their guides have twelve instruction sheets. This work seems to be what the Lord was calling for in England. One day, I might manage an English translation![62]

In an amusing sidenote, Roger Cunningham was so fired up after interpreting the preaching at the final Sunday evening's meeting that he continued to preach in his dreams that night. When he reached the appeal, inviting people to receive Christ as their Saviour, he began talking in his sleep, much to the amusement of a fellow minister who was sharing the same bedroom. "That was a powerful appeal you made in the night, brother," Eduardo said to him next morning. "I put *my* hand up!"

ℳ ℳ ℳ ℳ ℳ ℳ ℳ

After the crusade, there were another couple of miracles that we became aware of. One concerned a lady—a member of our church—whom I visited. Maria couldn't attend the services, so she liked me to come to her house, read the Bible and pray with her for the salvation of her family. They lived in a particularly poor part of the city, where a gutter smelling strongly of sewage ran alongside the unmade street.

When her husband Cayetano was first told I was coming, he left the house before I arrived, while their 18-year-old son Roberto shut himself in his bedroom. On my third visit, Cayetano didn't leave the house but stayed in the kitchen instead. This time, Roberto left his bedroom door open while Maria and I talked. On the visit after that, Roberto's door was again open, and this time, Cayetano appeared.

"Have you ever eaten an ají?" he asked with a grin.

I didn't know what an ají was, so he showed me a tiny red pepper.

"Try it," he said. "It's good."

---

[62] I have translated the simple Bible studies into English, and they can be downloaded free of charge from the publisher's website https://www.booksforlife.today.

Naïvely, I put it in my mouth and bit it. Aargh! My mouth was on fire. It was like swallowing a red-hot poker! Cayetano couldn't contain his glee. Unfortunately, Chileans have a great sense of humour, and they love to tease their friends. I don't think he meant it maliciously, for he did have the grace to fetch a cup of water for me. But the ají incident broke the ice. The next time I visited them, Cayetano was there to greet me.

"Come with me," he said. "I want to show you what I've been doing. I've put an electric light in the kitchen." I followed him in, and sure enough a light bulb was suspended above our heads. Dangling from its place on the ceiling, a couple of wires stretched to the wall, where they were fixed in place with sticky tape and then found their way down to a rickety power socket. Cayetano looked at me with pride on his face.

"Switch it on," he said.

I couldn't help wondering whether this was going to be another ají experience but ten times as bad. But hey! People did worse things to Jesus. I bravely pressed the switch, and the light came on. I survived.

"Mind you," Cayetano confided, "I had to have a few drinks before I was brave enough to switch it on the first time."

Both Cayetano and Roberto were in church on the Sunday after the evangelistic crusade finished. Cayetano asked José if he could say a word, and he addressed the congregation.

"Roberto and me used to fight a lot, fight real bad," he said. "But my wife told us to go and listen to the English preachers, so we did." He turned towards his son.

"Roberto, I want you to know I am very, very sorry for all the fights we have had. Things will be different from now on."

He walked over to Roberto's seat, asked him to stand up, and gave him the most enormous, loving hug!

❧ ❧ ❧ ❧ ❧ ❧ ❧

Valeria Zuñiga—the young lady whose hearing was restored at the crusade—had a father who had been diagnosed with gallstones. For some reason, the hospital in Punta Arenas was unable to operate on them, and consequently, Hector was booked in for an operation in Santiago. Before he left, Valeria asked José to pray for him.

José replied, "The Lord healed you. Why don't you pray for your dad? God will answer your prayers just as well as mine."

So she did.

Her father was admitted into hospital on January 1st, 1981, but nothing was done to him for a whole week. All that time, he kept declaring, "The Lord will heal me." On January 8th, everything was ready for him in the operating theatre. A last-minute X-ray was taken, but it revealed that there was nothing wrong with him anymore. The operation was suspended, and Hector returned to his ward, which he shared with six other men.

In the afternoon, Roger Cunningham visited him. I didn't even know that Hector was in hospital until the following day when I went to stay with Roger and he told me the story:

"Your friend Hector Zuñiga has been such a blessing to us," Roger told me. "I went to see him yesterday. He wanted me to meet the other men in his ward. 'This is so-and-so,' he said. 'Jesus has healed him. This is so-and-so: Jesus has healed him, too. And this man over here—Jesus has taken the pain away from him.'"

Hector had been praying with them all, and the Lord had answered his prayers for three of them.

Roger prayed with the other three men before he left. I'd love to know what the medics made of it all!

Hector returned to Punta Arenas without being operated on, and so far as I know, he never needed an operation.

Chapter 21. Scenes of Southern Chile

I was visiting Roger that January because we both had to attend the annual assembly of the Methodist Church in Angol, a town to the south of the capital. However, a Chilean pastor named Sergio Loyola had invited me to preach in his church in Chillán, midway between Santiago and Angol. So on January 10th 1981, I travelled 250 miles south from Santiago in a beautiful double-decker bus to Chillán.

The region around Chillán is extremely fertile: rice, peaches, tomatoes, grapes, apricots, oranges, maize and sugar beet grow there. On the Saturday night, I spoke on the Holy Spirit; on Sunday morning, I led a Bible study; and on Sunday night, I preached an evangelistic sermon, with several responding to the appeal. I earned my keep!

On Monday afternoon, Sergio took me further south to Talca, where the Methodist Church had established a congregation in one of the poorest quarters—what we would call a social housing development. 900 families lived in little wooden houses, none of which had piped water. The people filled buckets, empty bottles and old paint cans from standing taps in the unpaved streets. Women washed their families' clothes at the taps, surrounded by a sea of mud in winter. Children swam in a deep stream full of rubbish and human effluent.

Only 100 of the 900 families had regular employment, yet practically every home had a television. Three of them even had a colour TV! These were paid for on credit, which the enterprising householders recovered by charging small fees to their neighbours to come in and watch.

A community centre financed by World Vision formed part of the church's work there. Methodist workers assisted the poorest children by providing extra schooling, food and activities for 6-year-olds to 14-year-olds. Some parents attended classes in health and home craft.

※ ※ ※ ※ ※ ※ ※

Another 100 miles south, and I was in Angol for the Annual Assembly of the Methodist Church, the principal purpose of my journey. The Church had an agricultural college there. Once again, the beauty of Chilean trees overwhelmed me: an incredible variety, tall, lovely and—so far as I could tell—disease-free. The Lord is a marvellous creator.

José was reappointed superintendent of the Austral District, which was a relief. A ministerial student, Roberto, was appointed to help us in Punta Arenas for his year of practice, which was marvellous.

After a bad opening day involving some disagreements and arguments, a handful of us decided to meet to pray about it. At about 10:00 p.m. we went outside and found a secluded spot surrounded by tall poplars and elms. The night was pleasantly warm, and a bright moon shone down. We sat in a circle on the ground, surrounded by twinkling fireflies. It was peaceful and beautiful—so very beautiful! We were united in our praise of the One who brought it all into being.

We continued in prayer until midnight, except for one point when three women joined us. They had heard us praying, got out of bed, dressed, and came to join us. Looking back now, we must have been praying very loudly! Two of the women gave their lives to Jesus for the first time, so presumably they were locals rather than delegates to the conference!

After our prayers, the conference improved. The following night, 14 people joined our unofficial prayer meeting, and the next day, the conference improved even more. The service on the final Sunday evening was so full of the Holy Spirit that it didn't end until 11:15 p.m!

※ ※ ※ ※ ※ ※ ※

Next day, travelling another 200 miles south by bus, I reached the town of Osorno, photographing a smoking volcano on the way!

A young pastor from Osorno had been in Punta Arenas during the crusade. His name was Miguel Pérez, and he was to become extremely significant in my story. Squatly solid, Miguel had thick black Chilean hair but no eyelashes, which meant he had to wear tinted glasses in sunlight.

After the final meeting in the theatre, Miguel had asked Don Double if he would be willing another year to come to Osorno to preach. Don said he would be delighted to come if Miguel would organize everything with the churches there. And so it was that in Osorno, I met representatives of fifty churches whom Miguel had brought together to discuss inviting Don Double and Mike Darwood to lead a mission there next time they were in Chile. Miguel took me to a beautiful open-air stadium in a park and said they could easily bring 6000 or 7000 people together to hear the Gospel there. We discussed some of the arrangements that would be needed.

Another 63 miles south finally brought me to the town of Puerto Montt, from where a plane would take me home. I had wanted to travel to Puerto Montt by steam train, the one that Ann had seen in her vision in 1970, but I arrived at the railway station in Osorno just too late to catch the 'Rapido' from Santiago, which was five and a half hours late! Rather than wait another two hours for the 'Express' (which quite possibly might not have arrived until the following day), I took a bus to Puerto Montt. After waiting an hour at the Puerto Montt railway station, I photographed the arrival of the 'Rapido': we had passed it on the way! As it steamed slowly into the station, its long-suffering passengers triumphantly waved out of the windows at the cheering crowds who had been patiently waiting on the platform for half a lifetime to greet them.

The plane flight from Puerto Montt to Punta Arenas was breathtaking. For once, there was no cloud, and below us, I could see all the islands, several thousand islands, like the pieces of an unmade jigsaw puzzle, stretching into the distance as far as the eye could see. Some were flat, some hilly, and some mountainous: some perhaps only a few square miles in size, others hundreds of square miles: some bare, some with trees, and, after the first 100 miles, all uninhabited. Further south, glaciers appeared, thousands of square miles of ice breaking off at the edges of lakes and seashores into tiny slabs of white confetti floating in the water. I was so overcome, I cried!

And then we reached the Torres del Paine, or Paine Towers. At the southern extremity of the Andes, there are several towering pinnacles of rock; the jagged teeth of some petrified prehistoric leviathan, petrifying anyone who dares to scale them. They are famous among the world's mountaineering community, and form the focal point of the Paine National Park. Usually, clouds hid them from the air, but the sky was crystal clear that day.

Some Japanese tourists on the plane became very excited. Several of them left their seats and went to the aircraft's left side to get a better view and take photos. The pilot, realizing this was an unusual opportunity, and wanting to do what he could to help, voluntarily tipped the plane onto its side so that we could look directly down onto the mountains. When I realized what was happening, I promptly joined the tourists and others with my camera. Nearly all of us were crowded together on the left-hand side of the plane, excitedly photographing God's extraordinary handiwork!

This was not a charter flight but a routine scheduled flight from Santiago. The pilot's action was crazy, dangerous, and wonderful! Where else could such an action have taken place than in this uninhibited, disorganized, unreliable, generous, hospitable and extraordinarily beautiful country?

I was now absolutely, head-over-heels, in love with Chile.

Chapter 22. An Encounter with an Angel?

Tierra del Fuego is the large, roughly triangular island at the foot of South America, separated from the mainland by the Straits of Magellan.

At the beginning of February 1981, a family who lived on the island offered us the use of their house while they were on holiday on the mainland.

The Methodist Overseas Division in England had recently paid for me to buy a car, so it was our first proper outing in it when we all set off for our summer holiday. It was a 200-mile drive along the south coast of mainland Chile to the point where a car ferry could take us across to the island, and then a further 30-mile drive on the island itself. As soon as we left Punta Arenas, we found ourselves on an unmade gravel road. The five of us crunched along it for mile after mile without encountering a single other vehicle, and we passed only two or three houses all the way. What would have happened if we'd had a puncture or a breakdown, I do not know, for we had no mobile phones in those days.[63]

It is thought that early explorers of the region named Tierra del Fuego 'The Land of Fire' because of the many fires the inhabitants burned to keep themselves warm. Once, like Easter Island and the Falkland Islands, it was covered in trees, but in 1981 there was scarcely a tree to be seen in the part that we visited, only miles and miles of undulating grassland and the occasional flock of emu-like rheas.

The tiny settlement of Cerro Sombrero had one general store and a free sports centre for the oil workers who lived there. The sports centre was almost the only attraction. It included an Olympic-sized swimming pool in which our

---

[63] The coastal road has since been paved.

daughter learned to swim. She loves to tell her friends that she learned to swim in Tierra del Fuego!

Relieved from church responsibilities for a while, I had time to think about the coming year.

After Ann was first filled with the Holy Spirit, we were keen to tell as many people as possible about the reality of Jesus's promised helper. As a result, church members in Norfolk and Somerset received the Spirit by faith in Jesus's promises, opening up their lives to new peace and joy and love. They were helped in this by an influential new book entitled *Nine O'Clock in the Morning*,[64] which I lent to people.

I wanted to do something similar in Punta Arenas, so I had written a small book entitled *Tell Me About the Holy Spirit*, which Charlotte had offered to translate into Spanish. I was eagerly looking forward to sharing my new book with our church members, and with other churches in the city as well.

[February 5th, 1981]

> *I shall ask José to schedule three meetings a week with me and the student for sharing and prayer, and to plan together for the next day or two. I shall visit the pastors of all the churches in Punta Arenas and arrange for us to come together once a month to get to know each other better and pray for one another and the needs in each other's churches. Each month, I'll give one pastor a chance to answer the questions, "What my church means to me," and "What the Lord has been teaching me."*

I was beginning to take on a wider role of leadership.

¥ ¥ ¥ ¥ ¥ ¥ ¥

One day, while on holiday on the island, I went for a walk. I watched some otters playing around in a stream of sparklingly clear water. They took no notice of me. I found some berries

---

[64] *Nine O'Clock in the Morning*. Dennis J Bennett, Coverdale House Publishers, 1970.

similar to blueberries, and I ate some. That evening, someone told me they were calafates, and that anyone who ate a calafate would return to Tierra del Fuego one day. It seemed that more than one place in Patagonia wanted visitors to return. Perhaps in the Resurrection, when Jesus comes back to establish his 1000-year kingdom, I shall plant trees there once more.

As a favour to the kind people who had lent us their house, I decided to clean up their backyard. Spotting a sizeable empty oil drum, I put all the rubbish that would burn into it and set fire to it. Our three-year-old watched with interest what I was doing.

※ ※ ※ ※ ※ ※ ※

By February 11th, we were back home in Punta Arenas. I found a letter waiting for us from Jerry Wright, a man we had met in Aylsham and whom I had introduced to Jesus.

"Lay down what you are doing for the Lord," he wrote. "If it is his will, he will give it back to you, perhaps with a clearer vision." Whatever could his words mean? Were they really from the Lord? It must have taken him a great deal of courage to write that.

I might have fallen in love with Chile, but Ann, my wife, didn't share my feelings about it at all. When I first met her all those years ago, she used to suffer from nervous indigestion. Now, once again, her indigestion had returned, along with headaches. Thankfully, she had experienced no post-natal depression after the birth of our last two boys, but now it seemed she was beginning to struggle again. She had become unnecessarily anxious about the children's health; she was taking unusual care in hygiene and food preparation; and she was trying to order every day's events, growing upset when that order was broken for any reason. She was missing Julian in England, and she wasn't sleeping well at night.

However, our three-year-old Zachary brought all this to an end on Thursday, February 19th, 1981. It was one of the most dramatic days of our life. For reasons I'll explain shortly, I was in the city centre, while Zakky was at home, deciding to be helpful. From a brief conversation with him after the event, I have a good idea of what was going through his little mind...

I am just tall enough to see into the waste bin in the kitchen. I poke the lid open to see what's inside. There is some rubbish in it. I will help Daddy. I know where he keeps the matches to light the big things that keep us warm. The matches are in a drawer. I can reach it! Yes, here they are. I saw how to strike a match when we were on holiday. I'll see if I can do it. I go over to the waste bin. I rub a match along the side of the box. Ooh! The match is alight! I drop it into the bin. Yes, the rubbish is burning up nicely. Daddy will be pleased with me for helping him...

The flames are getting very big. I don't think they should be so big. I'd better stop them. I blow hard on them like Mummy blew out the candles on her birthday cake. But they don't stop. I blow as hard as I can. But they are still getting bigger. Something is wrong. The flames are coming out now. I must tell someone. Mummy is asleep in her bedroom. She has a sleep in the afternoon. She won't want me to wake her. Sometimes, she gets cross. What shall I do? It is getting so hot in here. Have I been naughty? I am scared. I am very scared. What shall I do?

The previous day, Wednesday, February 18th, I'd received a telegram from England telling me that my father had died. I knew he had been seriously ill, but I hadn't felt able to go home and visit him.

That same Wednesday evening, I was at a service at one of the three Methodist churches in the city. It was in Fitzroy, near where we lived. Fitzroy was named after the British admiral Robert Fitzroy, who explored this part of the world. He was the captain of HMS Beagle on Darwin's famous voyage.

At the end of the service, I was asked to say a closing prayer. I found myself praying, "Father, we know we need not fear anything, not even an earthquake or a fire, for whatever happens to us, we are secure in your hands if we keep close to you, for you are ordering all things in love for our good." I had never prayed such a prayer in English, let alone in Spanish. Where did that come from?

The next day, I was in the city centre making arrangements to travel back to England for my father's funeral. I had to visit the International Police to ask about recovering my passport from Santiago. It had been there for several months while our applications for permanent residence were being processed. The police assured me that I could collect it on my way back to England. They told me where to go. Good! I could fly home on Friday afternoon.

I was about to return to our house and start packing when I realized I needed to visit a travel agent to book a flight. But after a few steps in the new direction, something stopped me. *"My times are in your hand,"* a voice in my head said. It was a verse from a psalm. For some reason, that verse had been going round in my head for several days. I stopped walking. I stood still on the pavement, with traffic and people passing by. Once more, I prayed to God:

"Lord, my times are in your hand. Shall I go to the travel agent now to arrange a flight back to England, or leave it until tomorrow and go home now?"

Somehow, the Lord's answer came into my head—not merely a thought, but words—"Go home. Ann needs you."

Our new car was being serviced at a garage: it needed some tender loving care following the return trip to Tierra del Fuego. So, in no particular hurry, I went to catch a bus home. The moment I reached the bus stop, a black collective taxi drove up and stopped in front of me. The driver leant towards the open window and said, "You are going to Fitzroy?" Fitzroy was a tiny neighbourhood on the city's western edge, only a few short streets. How did he know I was going there? "Get in!" he told me.

I did as I was told. For once, I was the only passenger.

The drivers of 'colectivos' had to keep to their designated bus route, and they usually drove quite slowly because passengers could flag them down anywhere, not only at bus stops. This driver was different.

What is happening? He is going too fast. And this is not the way the bus goes. I think he's taking me directly to Fitzroy! I grip the edge of the seat. He is going way too fast: it's dangerous! Thank goodness there's no traffic in our way: that's strange...

In next to no time, we reached the end of our street. I got out, and the man drove off before I could pay him! Puzzled, I walked the short distance to our house, and there I had a shock. The front door was open and smoke was billowing out. Our lovely two-storey house was on fire!

Chapter 23. Saved!

My first thought was that everyone must have got out of the house, for when I called, "Is anyone there?", there was no response. I retreated into the front yard and put my bag down in what seemed to be a safe place. I had no phone to summon a fire brigade, and I wouldn't have known how to do it in any case. But I had to be sure the house was empty. So I cried, "Help me, Jesus!", clapped my handkerchief over my mouth, and re-entered the house. Already, there was so much smoke that I couldn't see anything.

This time, I heard my daughter's voice. "We're upstairs."

"Come down. The house is on fire!"

I ran up the stairs, found her on the landing and helped her down. As we reached the ground floor, flames from the open-plan dining room singed her eyebrows. We made it outside to safety.

"Is anyone else in the house?" I asked.

"Joseph was with me. We were playing in our bedroom. I told him to follow me."

The internal hardboard walls of the house were insulated with slabs of polystyrene, which by now were fully on fire. Whatever remained of the staircase had disappeared in a pall of oily black chemical smoke. I started to climb the stairs again and bumped into Joseph in the darkness. Our five-year-old had come nearly all the way down on his own! I tucked him under my arm like a rugby ball and turned to face the flames. I didn't know if the lowest stairs could still support us, or even whether they were still there. But in rugby, there is only one way to score a try. You go for the touchline, regardless of whoever is or is not in the way. Shielding him from the flames as best I could, I touched down in the open air with my small son safe and sound.

Ann was now calling for help from the bedroom window upstairs. She had been fast asleep, taking an afternoon siesta after a morning of teaching at the British School. The smell of smoke had woken her up.

"What shall I do?" she called out.

"Come down the stairs."

"I can't. They are all in flames."

"Then you must jump. I'll try to catch you."

"I can't do that!"

I looked around for inspiration. Through the smoke, I saw a short ladder leaning against the wall of the house. Had it always been there? It was too short to reach her, but a neighbour appeared, and together we lifted the ladder to the level of the bedroom window. Ann clambered down. She fell near the bottom and hurt her ankle, but she was safe.

By now, other neighbours were on the scene.

"Where's Zakky?" I asked the world at large. I was terrified that the little one was unconscious in the heart of the fire, burning or burnt to death. The air was thick with smoke; my eyes were streaming. I heard and smelt the crackling of burning wood, and knew I couldn't reenter such an inferno.

"He might be with la Abuelita—the Granny," someone said. The widow Carmen Barria had become a dear friend to all our children, especially our youngest son. Perhaps he had gone to her house for some reason: it was just across the road. I knocked on her front door, and Zachary himself opened it, safe and sound. Praise God!

And then I remembered Charlotte Richardson who lived with us and had also been in her room. Why had we heard nothing from her? A girl in the street told me she had seen 'la señorita Charlotte' jump from her bedroom window. Someone else told me that an ambulance came and took her to the hospital. She had hit her head on some railings as she fell, but at least she was being cared for.

We took shelter in Carmen Barria's house, all except Emerald, who stayed outside with a friend because she had a lot of smoke in her lungs and wanted to be in the open air. Some of the onlookers expressed amazement at how calm and peaceful I was. I *was* calm and peaceful, now that I knew my family was safe! The smoke and flames hadn't touched me, nor the trauma of entering a burning house and losing many of my possessions. It was like the Bible says, *"When you walk through fire, you shall not be burned, and the flame shall not consume you. For I am the Lord your God, the Holy One of Israel, your Saviour."*[65]

There was now an enormous crowd of onlookers in the street. Two or three fire engines arrived, along with police officers and some marines trained in firefighting. Some reporters and photographers turned up. Next day, there would be a front-page report in the principal local newspaper claiming that all six of the city's fire brigades had come to rescue us.

The firemen who did turn up put out the fire and saved some of our most precious possessions. But it was the Lord who truly saved my family by commissioning a supernatural taxi-driving angel to bring me back to the house just in time. I don't just believe that angels exist: now I *know* they do!

Some medics insisted on taking us all to hospital for a check-up. In Chile, the pastors of registered church denominations and their families were entitled to free medical help, and I was so grateful.

The following day, I returned to the scene of devastation. Our kind neighbour met me and told me that he had been inside and had taken a few things out for safekeeping, including Ann's little stock of jewellery. I looked around the kitchen where the fire had undoubtedly started. All that remained of the two internal walls were charred wooden frameworks with gaping holes through them. The floor was black with smoke and the remains of burnt lino.

Everything in the kitchen was burnt except in one small corner. Here, there was still wallpaper on the wall, surprisingly untouched by the fire. And in that self-same corner, on the

---

[65] Isaiah 43:2-3

smoke-blackened floor, there were two light-coloured rectangular patches that must have been protected from the smoke by two objects standing there during the blaze. Whatever were they? They weren't there now, so my neighbour must have taken them. And then I remembered. They were two 5-litre plastic cans filled with paraffin for our paraffin stove. Miraculously, the inferno had bypassed that one small, explosive corner in the self-same room where the fire had started. Startled, I recalled my prayer on the Wednesday evening: *"Not even an earthquake or a fire..."*

Although much of what we owned was destroyed—even our empty tea chests in the loft didn't wholly escape—a few things, amazingly, did survive. All our essential documents—our birth and marriage and degree certificates; records of our childhood achievements and our children's achievements; our bankbooks, money and identification papers—these were all kept in an old leather briefcase. While the briefcase itself was ruined and could never be used again, it had perfectly protected all its contents: they were not even smoke-damaged.

Our family photos, going back to our childhood, had also survived—pictures of ourselves, our children, our relatives, and many people who had become important to us during our lifetime. The covers of the albums were spoilt, but somehow, the photos themselves survived intact. Most astonishingly of all, a cassette recording of my father narrating his life story still worked. It was doubly precious now that he had gone. He could no longer speak to us, but his voice lived on.

It didn't matter about the washing machine, the refrigerator, our furniture or even our clothes and toys. They could all be replaced, but the tangible memories of our lives in the form of certificates, photos and recordings of how we grew up and of the people who made us what we are—these could never have been replaced.

After the fire, I said to my 10-year-old daughter, "We are like Jesus now. He didn't have much either."

"We still have our faith in God," she replied. "That's the most important thing."

❧ ❧ ❧ ❧ ❧ ❧ ❧

There was a member of the British community named Peggy Fell. She owned a substantial house close to the Central Methodist Church, but was at her summer residence somewhere in the countryside. Someone must have told her what had happened to us, for she returned to the city that same day to offer us the use of her town house until we could find somewhere permanent for ourselves. A Canadian girl who had been staying with Peggy remained with us in her house and even cooked for us! Ann was confined to bed for a few days because of her twisted ankle. Emerald soon recovered from the smoke, and God helped all three of our children to sleep peacefully that night. We stayed in Peggy's house for two and a half weeks.

It's amazing how God can bring good out of evil. He did have a long-term purpose in allowing our house to catch fire, but the good that immediately emerged from it was the overwhelmingly generous, sacrificial, and astonishing help that our neighbours and church family extended towards us all. They made us feel so loved, as though we were the most important people in the world!

While we were at the hospital, neighbours rescued our surviving belongings and stacked them up in their yards for safe keeping. The next day, church members hired a truck and took everything to the church hall to clean it up. For days, they were washing crockery and cutlery, clothes, bedding, soft toys and anything else that remained usable.

People visited us in our borrowed home, phoned us, and gave us things almost every hour. On the Saturday, Charlotte had 17 visitors, and Ann had almost as many. Ann at last plucked up the courage to speak to them in Spanish and discovered that she could! Emerald, who lost all her dresses and most of her other clothes, was given all kinds of things by her friends to replace them. People gave us toys for the children and clothes for all of us.

We received a box of groceries, some homemade jam and some magazines in English. We were given beds, chairs, tables, a wardrobe, a refrigerator, a gas cooker, a gas stove, a tea service and even a colour TV. Someone gave me a cheque for £250.[66] Someone else gave us a wall plaque—a little late!— that said in English, "Bless this house, O Lord, we pray; keep it safe by night and day." Wherever did that come from?

For days and days, José helped me restore the smoke-damaged furniture that survived the fire; sanding it all back to clean wood and then varnishing it back to perfection. After that, he helped me paint every one of our remaining smoke-damaged tea chests so that we could use them again if we ever returned to England. What a blessing that man, his wife, and all our friends and neighbours were to us!

🌿 🌿 🌿 🌿 🌿 🌿 🌿

The night of the fire, our house agent visited us and said he had another house available if we were interested. It was the only suitable house he had, on one of the city's main residential streets, but it was a little more expensive than our first house. We discussed it with Charlotte, and she said she'd be happy to pay the extra out of her earnings at school, as her contribution to the rent.

[Sunday February 22nd, 1981]

> *It has a large lounge/living room with a gas heater and a large open fireplace; four bedrooms, each with built-in wardrobes and cupboards, and the biggest with a new gas heater; a bathroom with a heater and bidet; a kitchen and breakfast room; and a large loft with lights in it. It has a small garden full of cabbages, lettuces, rhubarb, gladioli and other flowers; a hen house and chicken run;*

---

[66] Now worth £1000

and a storehouse as big as a bedroom, which the children can use as a playroom. There is a driveway with room for three cars, a wood store, and flower borders with lupins (one of my favourite flowers) on two sides of the house. It has lino throughout and lace curtains on every window.

Wow! What a blessing!

[Monday February 23rd, 1981]

We feel such a sense of our Father's care, especially in saving everybody's life, that it is impossible to feel sad. One thing the Lord has done has been most wonderful: he has brought people in the church together—together with each other and with us. Everybody feels sure that what has happened has and will have inestimably good results for the church's life as a whole.

Back in Fitzroy, there had been a poster on the wall above our bed. It read, 'Go out among the people and light a fire of love within their hearts.' Somehow, we had done that. I would have preferred it if the Lord hadn't enabled us to do it in such a traumatic way, but I trusted that he knew best. We had all been saved, and I wasn't going to complain!

And then I recalled the letter from Jerry about laying down what I was doing. Was it only about the fire, or was there more 'laying down' to come?

151

Chapter 24. A Stunning and Unwelcome End

On March 6th, just before we moved into our new house, I wrote a long letter to our contacts in the Methodist Church Overseas Division in London.[67]

I asked permission for us all to return to England for a short break. I wanted to spend some time with my now-widowed mother, Ann wanted to spend some time with Julian, and while she didn't want to leave Chile for ever, she felt she needed a complete break from it before starting there again. And she wanted to set Emerald up with her new school uniform, because the Methodist Church had agreed that Emerald could become a boarder at a Methodist school in England in September. We had the idea that until then she could live with one of several families we knew, attending a local primary school while the rest of us returned to Chile. I offered to pay the return fares for the two boys.

In response, the newly appointed Latin American secretary, Ivy McGhee, came to Chile. She met the new Bishop, Isaías Gutierrez, in Santiago, and then she spent two days with us in Punta Arenas. It was a weird visit. Unusually, it rained almost continuously, and somehow it felt as though a veil of sadness was covering the city.

We were sitting with her around a table in our beautiful new house when Roberto, the student, came to visit us. He was an earnest young man with a thin face and a shock of black hair.

"Good morning, Pastor," he said. "Good morning, Pastora Ann. And good morning...?"

---

[67] I often used to write long letters. Nowadays, my letters are mostly shorter emails, so I write long books instead.

"This lady is called Ivy," I responded. "She has come from London to visit us."

"From London? We are pleased to have you here, señora. I hope you are enjoying your stay in this beautiful city."

I interpreted what he said to Ivy. She gave him a non-committal smile.

"So why are you here, Roberto?" I asked.

"Ah, yes! We understand that you may be returning to England for a while, so I've brought you a schedule of preaching and Sunday school teaching appointments. We've tried to fit in as many appointments for you as possible in the next three weeks before you leave."

I stared at him in wordless horror. I still hadn't recovered emotionally from our recent trauma in the fire and from moving house with six people twice in three weeks. The thought of preparing new sermons and teaching material while packing up for us to return to England pitchforked me into a despairing heap of frustration.

"I'm so sorry, Roberto. I really can't manage anything like that now. I have to say no. Please find someone else."

Surprised and disappointed, Roberto took his leave. Ivy gave me a thoughtful look. The veil of sadness sank a little lower around us. I was astounded at the church's lack of understanding.

❧ ❧ ❧ ❧ ❧ ❧ ❧

Ivy spoke to her colleagues in London and reported back to us.

"It's been agreed that you can return to England as you asked. We will pay your fares. But you must know that whenever a missionary family returns to England, for whatever reason, their posting is reviewed, and it is not necessarily renewed. This means that before you leave, you will have to pack everything you have ready to be shipped back to England in case it's decided that you are not to return here."

As usual, we talked to the Lord. He told us through prophecy that he would swiftly sort everything out, and sure enough, he did! Within a week, we received our passports, which we had been waiting for since November following our application for permanent residence. We obtained new identity cards in 24 hours, even though the lady who issued them had said would take at least three weeks. We booked our seats on a plane from Punta Arenas to Santiago and another from Santiago to England: they were the last five seats available on both aircraft! We bought new suitcases for the journey, and in our 24 remaining tea chests we packed up everything else we owned that would go into them, in case for some awful reason we were not allowed to return.

All our family were now permanent residents of Chile, including Julian, who was given this status through an administrative error, even though he was in England. In the future, we'd be able to come and go freely between Chile and Britain without having to apply for visas. At last, my life's calling to be a Christian foreign missionary had become a settled reality!

Ann and I hadn't liked Ivy much, but I guess that wasn't her fault. We'd been told that her visit was to assess the situation in Punta Arenas, in order to make a decision about our future there. But somehow, both Ann and I had felt that, in reality, the visit was little more than a formality: it was merely to confirm a decision that had already been made.

Sure enough, the day before we left Punta Arenas, I received a telegram. It informed me that the executive committee in London had recommended terminating our appointment to Chile. Of what use was our permanent residence status now?

❧ ❧ ❧ ❧ ❧ ❧ ❧

Because of the short notice, there was time only for one more brief meeting with the church before we left. Several people were in tears when I explained the decision. It seemed so wrong, so very, very wrong.

Three days earlier, we had heard of a revival in the Methodist Church in Puerto Natales, the nearest town. 150

people had been converted, and they had asked me to produce 200 more copies of the Bible study booklets for new Christians that I had written the previous year.

Two days earlier, Charlotte had finished her translation of a book on the work of the Holy Spirit that I had written, and I knew of no one in the Central Methodist Church who could introduce the teaching of this book to study groups in the church.

The very day that we left, a letter from Don Double arrived, informing me that he and Mike Darwood would be coming to Punta Arenas the following year for a whole week's mission. Don asked me if I would act as the local coordinator again. Added to all this, the English-speaking community would now be without an ordained minister, and the monthly services of Holy Communion in St James's church would have to cease. Where was God in all this?

An old hymn begins, 'God moves in a mysterious way, his wonders to perform.' It was hard to think of anything more mysterious than what he was doing just then. What a mess! How could this disaster ever have been his will? "What are you doing, Lord?" I wanted to cry, but I was too numb in my spirit to utter a word.

'Lay down what you are doing for the Lord,' Jerry had written. 'If it is his will, he will give it back to you, perhaps with a clearer vision.'

How could that possibly happen?

[Part of a letter to me from Isaías Gutiérres Vallejos, Bishop of the Methodist Church of Chile, April 30th, 1981, translated.]

...but we can be sure that the Lord will continue to guide our lives, in light and shade, in winter and in spring, and we can experience the joy of his presence and friendship, whatever our circumstances. Your support has been valuable, and we thank God and all of you for it. Your possible return to Chile needs to be guided attentive to the unity of your family, which we would never want to break, and

in consequence we commend all your future to the wisdom of the Lord.

He added: '*Your coming to Chile has opened a marvellous channel of contact with the beloved English Methodist Church, a contact which we would want to maintain and cultivate.*'

Another door God had unlocked through me. That was something, at least.

❧ ❧ ❧ ❧ ❧ ❧ ❧

We were never clear why the Methodist Church decided to terminate our appointment. I think they felt that the Methodist Church in Chile had not looked after us as they should have, especially in the matter of the rent for our house.

I also think they were concerned about my ability to cope with my increasing responsibilities after Ivy's report on Roberto's visit to our house. In that regard, there was one thing I picked up at a later date—that there was a plan for José to be stationed elsewhere the following year, leaving me in complete charge of three churches on the mainland and a fourth tiny church in the town of Porvenir on the island of Tierra del Fuego. This would have involved managing property as well as people, and I'm not at all sure how well I could have coped with that.

Thirdly, I think Ivy sensed Ann's increasing struggle to cope with Chilean life in general. She had begun well with her teaching in the school, but after a year she had found it too stressful and had given it up.

Fourthly, the Bishop's letter hinted at concerns for our family, including perhaps our continuing separation from our oldest son.

Lastly, there was almost certainly an economic reason, one that my mother explained to me. She had some role in administering the collections for missionary work in the Methodist churches in Reading. The previous few years had seen high inflation rates, but the offerings had not kept up with rising costs, and supporting a family of five or six people abroad was not cheap.

At the time, I was heartbroken about having to leave my beloved Chile. God had so obviously brought us there—I'd assumed it would be for at least ten years, if not for the rest of our life—so to leave after only a year and a half simply didn't make sense. I couldn't see God's hand in it at all.

It has only been in the years since then that I have come to see the wisdom of some of the Church's concerns, and to be convinced of God's loving hand at work.

I believe he no longer wanted our family to be separated, with our two oldest children staying in England while the rest of us were in Chile. He knew what we found out only afterwards, that Julian had been unhappy living with my sister and brother-in-law. He was also concerned, I believe, about Ann's mental health, which he knew would become a serious issue again.

Although it astounds me, I now see that God considered the welfare of my little family even more important than my support for the revival in Puerto Natales, my teaching about the Holy Spirit, my coordination of a seven-day evangelistic crusade in the city and the loss of ministry in the city's Anglican Church. In God's eyes my family's needs came before all those other things. Yes! He cares more for us as individuals than for all the other 'big' things that we think are so important! Such love seems incredible, yet I believe it is true!

We returned to England on April 13th, 1981, in time to celebrate Easter. Although we had lived in Chile for only 17 months, it seemed like half a lifetime!

Chapter 25. Another Disappointment, and a Miracle of Provision

Despite being back in England, I remained officially employed until August 31st, but without any church responsibilities. Tony and Joyce Pitman, a married couple in one of my previous churches in Somerset, made an extraordinary sacrifice for us: they moved in with some equally sacrificial friends so that we could have the sole use of their own house rent-free for as long as we needed it!

[News and prayer letter no.7, June 1981]

On April 22nd, the Lord gave Ann a vision of a crossroads with a signpost pointing in three directions. Two days later, Graeme Jackson of the Overseas Division told me I had three choices: 1. To offer myself to the stationing committee meeting on May 21st for circuit work in Great Britain; 2. To be put on the President's list, which means being without an appointment or pay for one year while a decision is made about my future; or 3. To resign from the Methodist ministry and do something else.

After some thought and prayer, I chose the first option, to resume a ministry in Great Britain.

There was a Furlough Conference for missionaries temporarily back in Britain. I met Graeme at it to discuss where I might be stationed. He was a friendly man with an aura of scholarly efficiency.

"What are your thoughts about stationing, Arnold? Do you have any preferences about where to go?"

"I'd like it to be somewhere where there are good schools because our children are very bright. And if it's possible, I'd like us to be somewhere not too distant from Reading, where my mother lives. As you know, she's on her own now. Thirdly, there are some things I am good at and some things I am bad at. So I would love to be in a team ministry kind of circuit, where we could each take circuit responsibility for what we are good at and leave the other ministries to someone else.

"And there is one other thing. For years now, I have not conducted services of infant baptism, only services of dedication and thanksgiving for babies. It's never been a problem. When parents insisted on the traditional infant baptism service, my superintendent minister took the service. So it would have to be in a circuit where the superintendent would be willing to help out.

"Apart from those things, I think we'll both be happy to go wherever we are sent."

Graham's response was immediate.

"We can certainly do our best to meet your first three requirements, but not taking services of infant baptism is a definite problem. The Conferences of 1975 and 1977 decided that Methodist ministers must teach and practise infant baptism. Do you really have to insist on not baptizing babies? Is it that important to you?"

"Yes, it is. The word baptism means immersion. If I said to a baby, "I baptize you," and only sprinkled water on it, I would be lying. More importantly, the New Testament makes it clear that the purpose of baptism by immersion is for people to publicly express their repentance from a life of sin and their decision to follow Jesus as their Saviour and Lord. How can a baby do that?"

"I see. Well, that's not how most of us see it. But I'm willing to speak to the President of the Conference on your behalf if you would like me to."

"Yes, please. I don't want to leave the Methodist ministry unless I have to."

In July, Graham reported back to me. He had spoken to the new President of the Conference and to members of the

Stationing Committee. The President was adamant that if I would not 'baptize' babies, I would have to leave the Methodist ministry. Graham explained that it would be particularly difficult to reach any other decision, as it was only two years since another brother with the same opinions as mine was told he could not be stationed and was advised to resign from the ministry.

I had a big decision to make, a huge decision. How could I tell a congregation that they should live by the teaching of the Bible if I was doing something that I was convinced was not what it taught? Whether I was right or wrong, I would be acting against my conscience, which the Bible says is an extremely dangerous thing to do.[68] Yet if I resigned from the ministry, I would have neither a job nor a home, for apart from when we were in Chile, our house had always been provided for us as part of my employment arrangements. No job, no house, no fortune in the bank, and a family of six people to provide for. We needed supernatural guidance!

Ann and I held hands. Like little children, we asked our Father in heaven what to do. He showed Ann a vision of a tree stump, the stump of what had once been a great oak tree but had now been cut down. She understood this to represent the Methodist Church, which had once been a great institution, producing a revival of scriptural holiness throughout the British nation and probably rescuing it from a French-style political revolution, according to at least two historians.[69]

And now, like the tree stump, there was virtually nothing left of the Methodist Church, and there was no hope, in the vision at least, of its restoration. We were grateful for all that the

---

[68] 1 Corinthians 8:7-13

[69] The nineteenth century church historian William Lecky credited John Wesley with saving England from revolution, according to Samuel Shoemaker in his book *Extraordinary Living for Ordinary Men*, Zondervan, 1965. Cambridge historian Sir Herbert Butterfield expressed the same opinion in his book, *Christianity and History*, Harper Collins, 1949.

Church had given us, but neither of us wished to be part of a dying church any longer. And sorrowfully, we believed that the Lord didn't want us to remain in it either. Between 1981 and 2025, the Methodist Church in Britain lost two-thirds of its membership.

I informed Graham Jackson that I would leave the Methodist Church at the end of August.

☘ ☘ ☘ ☘ ☘ ☘ ☘

We were now totally in the hands of the Lord.

Pursuing an obvious route, I applied to the Baptist Union.

"Yes, of course we'd be willing to consider you for the ministry," someone official told me. "But you would have to complete two years of ministry training first."

Next, I applied for a ministerial assistant post in a big Anglican Church not far from where my sister lived. "We do have a vacancy, but to be honest, we are looking for a woman."

I looked at a map of England and decided that Nottingham was in the centre of the country. How wonderful it would be if I could begin a movement of spiritual revival there that would spread out nationwide in all directions from that city. And to my delight, I discovered that there was a suburb of Nottingham called Arnold. Was this where God intended me to be? I wrote to the minister of the Baptist Church in Arnold to ask if he was looking for an assistant, or if any church in the district was looking for someone. No openings were there either.

It looked as though I didn't have the key to open this particular door. All I felt able to do was to follow the advice in the Bible: turn to God[70] and let him sort things out. '*Commit your way to the Lord; trust in him, and he will act,*' the Bible said.[71] That was the best thing I could do, the best of all.

---

[70] Isaiah 45:2
[71] Psalm 37:5

❧ ❧ ❧ ❧ ❧ ❧ ❧

A mile from where my sister then lived lay the village of Naphill, a couple of miles north of High Wycombe in the county of Buckinghamshire. In the centre of the village, proclaiming itself as 'Naphill Evangelical Church' was a church building. My sister was driving past it one day when she saw the pastor come out of his house to go into the adjacent church building. She managed to slow down and drive onto the forecourt before he disappeared. She ran up to him.

"Excuse me. I see this is an evangelical church. Is there some central body of evangelical churches or a directory of evangelical churches where I could find out if there is a church that needs a minister?"

"Why are you asking?"

"My brother has returned from a church in Chile, and he is looking for a post as a minister in a church here in England."

"Do you think your brother would be interested in coming here? I'm leaving in August, and I don't think the trustees have found anyone to replace me yet."

"I'm sure my brother would be interested. How would he have to apply?"

"He'd have to meet the trustees. Two of them live locally. If you give me your brother's phone number, I'll ask them to set up a meeting with him. What kind of church was he in?"

"It was the Methodist Church. But he had to leave it because he wouldn't baptize babies."

"Really? Then he'd like it here. The church has a baptistry."

❧ ❧ ❧ ❧ ❧ ❧ ❧

Soon afterwards, I had a long talk with a dear elderly trustee named Reg Griffiths, who asked me many questions and told me about the church.

"The property is owned and administered by three trustees. I am one of them, and I attend the services here. Another trustee attends a Brethren church in the town, and the third lives in Beaconsfield. A wealthy lady named Emma Grace founded the church in Victorian times. She built the original chapel on this site and bought a house in the village for a pastor. She invested enough money to provide him with a living, but most of that money has run out, so although you would have a house, we could not pay you.

"About twelve years ago, we sold the old manse and pulled down the old tin tabernacle. We built this new house and church from the sale proceeds and some of the remaining invested money. The house was supposed to have four bedrooms, but Mr Baker, the present minister, asked if one of the double bedrooms could be divided into two because he has four children. So the house has one double bedroom and four single ones. And, of course, a living room, dining room, kitchen and bathroom.

There are only about twelve of us in the congregation, but we want to see the church grow. What do you think?"

I was astonished. The house seemed to have been made for us—a bedroom for Ann and me and one each for the four children! Furthermore, while staying with my sister, Julian had passed a local authority entrance exam for the prestigious Royal Grammar School in High Wycombe. If I could pastor a church in the area, he could start at the school in September, together with a friend he had made who had passed the same exam. And because we'd live within a mile of my sister and her family, Emerald could attend junior school with her cousins. Lastly, I found out that the primary school Joseph would attend had a Christian headmistress, who said he would be in the same class as another Spanish-speaking boy whose family had just returned from Venezuela!

The church building had an office for my use, a kitchen, a baptistry and two full-size table tennis tables for our children and a future youth group. It all seemed like a perfect instance of answered prayer. Except that I would not be paid.

"With God, nothing will be impossible."[72]

I phoned my old friend David Watkins. He said he would speak to Dennis Patterson of the Come Back to God Campaign, the people who had prayed for me to be filled with the Holy Spirit ten years earlier. They didn't come up with any money, but they did offer us a lot of furniture, which we would need, for when Stanley Baker and his family moved out, the house would be empty.

Ann and I talked it over. Many of the things we had lost in the fire had been insured, and as a result, we had something like £5000 in the bank, worth about £20,000 in 2025. With care, it could keep us going for a year, for the house was rent-free. Perhaps in that time, if the Lord blessed my ministry, the numbers in the church would increase to the point at which the congregation could support us. It was a challenging scenario, but so much seemed right that we were sure it was of the Lord.

I had a further interview with the trustees. They had spoken to the congregation, who decided they could afford to pay me £10 a week to begin with and more if the church grew. I took a trial service there on July 26th and was invited to become the new pastor. We moved into our new home in time for me to start work on September 1st 1981, exactly as I would have done if I had still been a Methodist minister, in time for the start of the new school year.

---

[72] Luke 1:37

Chapter 26. Miracles of Finding, Depression and Miracle Housing

That summer in 1981, we all visited Keith and Pat Gilmore in Glastonbury. They were two of the people we had introduced to the Holy Spirit when we lived in Somerset, so it was good to have fellowship with them again.

Julian was playing with a frisbee in their garden, and somehow it got lost. He was getting upset, so I helped him to look for it, but I couldn't find it either. At last, I said, "Let's pray and ask Jesus to help us find it." We held hands, shut our eyes, and I said a sentence or two of prayer. When we opened our eyes, the frisbee was lying on the grass before us!

"Gosh! That was a quick answer to prayer!" Julian exclaimed.

But this was only number one on God's hide-and-seek agenda that summer.

❧ ❧ ❧ ❧ ❧ ❧ ❧

In August, we stayed with my mother in Reading for a few days. She had a large garden. At the end of the garden there was a plum tree bearing the most delicious ripe yellow plums I have ever tasted. Unfortunately, the wasps liked them too, so picking a plum was somewhat hazardous. There was also a damson tree on the lawn. It was loaded with so many ripe damsons that they were falling off the tree as we watched. We had great fun trying to catch them before they hit the ground.

By the plum tree, there was a shed full of toys for my mother's other, younger, grandchildren. They called her Granny Toys-in-the-Garden. Somehow, the key to the shed had been lost. After some fruitless searching for it, I prayed. I said, "Lord, you can see where that key is. Help me to see where it is, too." And somehow—and this was weird—I could see it out of sight under a rhubarb leaf. I lifted the leaf, and sure enough, there was the key! "Thank you, Lord!"

Number three was the big one. While we were staying with her, my mother was sad because she had lost the diamond from her engagement ring. Somehow, it had fallen out. Having already found two lost items, I prayed for help and began searching around the garden for it, but it was a big garden, and I swiftly realised that searching for such a small object was futile.

Zachary, then four years old, liked drains. I found him poking some sticks down a drain outside the kitchen. I told him to stop it, and I took the sticks out. As I was doing this, I noticed a lot of sludge in the drain, and I decided to clean it out as a favour to my mother. I donned some rubber gloves, took an old mug, and began bailing out the smelly sludge.

The drain was pretty deep, but I finally reached the bottom. I was about to tip the last bit of sludge out of the mug and into a bucket when I saw something sparkle in it. I gingerly spooned it out to be sure that it was what I thought it was, and it was! My mother was, of course, delighted. She said the diamond must have come out of her ring while she was washing some dishes in the sink, and it must have fallen down the plughole.

Why didn't the Lord show me where it was when I prayed, like he did on the two earlier occasions? Maybe he enjoyed playing hide-and-seek! But I am sure it was his Spirit who prompted me to clean out the drain.

Years later, I related the story of the ring to our congregation. Dorothy King, one of our members, was feeling upset because a day or two earlier she had lost all her rings. Hearing my story, she thought, "Perhaps the Lord will show me where they are." There and then, she asked the Lord to show her where her rings were, and he did! Sitting in church, she could see clearly where her lost rings were. After the service, she returned home and told her husband she knew where her rings were. He was the chairman of the local magistrates, and he was not a churchgoer.

"Ah, you've remembered where you put them, have you?" he said teasingly.

"No. In church, God showed me where they are."

Dorothy opened a cupboard in the kitchen and peered inside. At the back of it, almost out of sight, were her lost rings. She realised that her granddaughter, who had been visiting a few days earlier, must have hidden them there. Without the Lord's help, they might not have been found for years!

As a result of this miracle, Dorothy's husband agreed to start coming to church with her, but only to the parish church. So we lost one member of our congregation. But perhaps, through what happened, the Lord found a lost soul, too.

$\cancel{\hspace{1em}}$ $\cancel{\hspace{1em}}$ $\cancel{\hspace{1em}}$ $\cancel{\hspace{1em}}$ $\cancel{\hspace{1em}}$ $\cancel{\hspace{1em}}$ $\cancel{\hspace{1em}}$

And now back to the main story. The Naphill congregation welcomed us, and the children happily settled into their new home and schools. But after a month, I became seriously depressed. I was missing Chile and our precious friends there. I wrote a sad song in Spanish, accompanied by some despairingly sad piano music in the key of A minor.

In the farthest corner of the earth,
there I left my heart.
In the Land of Fire
my dreams awoke
and died.
We were as one, yet we were torn apart:
how could I have left you?
You wept with me,
as I weep now.
Such dreams! Such hopes!
Now, dust and ashes.

I kept bursting into tears, and my hands shook uncontrollably. I phoned my long-time mentor, Pastor Bob Hobbs, and explained what was happening.

He told me, "You are fighting God."

I thought about what he'd said, and I realized it was true. I was angry with God for allowing the events and decisions that had torn my life from Chile and from all the people there that I had grown to love so much. I had to repent of how I felt. I had to believe that it was out of God's love for me and my family that he had brought us back to England. So I asked him to forgive me for doubting his love for us, and I accepted that he had brought us back because he cared for us. And instantaneously, the depression ceased. The emotional wounds had been healed.

ꙮ ꙮ ꙮ ꙮ ꙮ ꙮ ꙮ

When I began my ministry in Naphill, the members comprised two youngish couples, the elderly trustee and his wife, and a collection of oldish people, mostly ladies. At the beginning, four or five older people came from the town every Sunday evening 'to support us', but in reality, their attendance merely gave me a second service to prepare for.

Very soon, one of the youngish couples left to join the London City Mission, so there was only the other couple to help Ann and me in active leadership. Ian Bickerstaffe worked locally in the RAF but was due to leave in May the following year. I was desperate for him and Susan to remain in the church by finding a house in the locality. I prayed they would find one in Naphill by June 1st, 1982. I prayed in detail for it and recorded in my diary what the Lord showed me.

Shortly before Ian left the RAF the following year, he began applying for jobs in High Wycombe, the local town. When he told me he had been offered two job interviews on the same day, I prayed about them. The Lord showed me that he would meet a Christian at the first of these interviews and be offered a job. I told Ian what the Lord had shown me, and it was precisely what happened. At the first interview, the interviewer was wearing a badge for some Christian organisation that Ian identified, so when he was offered a job there and then as an electronic tester, he accepted it on the spot.

Ian and Susan then had to find a house they could afford to buy.

In prayer the previous December, the Lord had shown me a house with three bedrooms, a living room large enough for a home group, a kitchen and dining room or a kitchen/diner, a shelter for the car, a garden with one or two fruit trees, a place for coats and 'something which I sensed, but couldn't clearly picture, in an entrance hall'. I wrote, 'Jesus said, "Whatever you ask the Father in my name, I will do it." So that was the house I asked God for.

But I didn't share it with Ian and Susan.

They went to view a house for sale close to the church. When they reported to me on their visit, I showed them what the Lord had shown me in prayer. We were all so excited. The house had three bedrooms, a large lounge, a kitchen and dining room, a garage, a garden with *four* fruit trees, a place for coats, and in the entrance hall… a downstairs toilet!

Unfortunately, homes in Naphill were considerably more expensive than those in the town. When Ian applied for a mortgage, the building society confirmed that the maximum mortgage they could offer on his new salary would leave them some £7000 short. We prayed about it, and Ian went to have another talk at the building society. This time, the lady said that the society had recently started a new low-start scheme for first-time buyers, under which she could offer more than needed and with lower initial repayments. I asked Ian to find out when the new scheme had started. It had started only five days earlier! Ian and Susan made an offer for the house, which was accepted.

It was the Lord's chosen house for them, and they became vital leaders in our small church.

❧ ❧ ❧ ❧ ❧ ❧ ❧

Initially, the church grew in numbers, and the Sunday offerings increased. The congregation doubled, and at one point, forty children were attending Sunday school.

However, in the four months leading up to February 1983, a couple wanting to take over the church caused a lot of dissension. In the end, the Lord removed them from the congregation, but several others left with them. After that, when our resident trustee and his wife moved to a retirement home, all that remained were three adults of a similar age to Ann and me, seven old ladies and an elderly man who was profoundly deaf and always fell asleep during the sermons.

By April 1983, my income was insufficient for our needs, and our money had run out. Ann tried supply teaching, but "Be quiet! Shut up! Sit down!" don't work so well in England as they did in Chile! She didn't find supply teaching easy, and admitted defeat.

So, with the trustees' approval, I looked for a part-time job. I immediately found one with an establishment named The Timber Research and Development Association, which supported the use and development of timber on behalf of the timber trade. TRADA was less than ten minutes' walk from our house, and a short interview secured a job for me as a part-time assistant groundsman.

Chapter 27. Almost Giving Up, and Return to Engineering

When I was first offered the pastorship in Naphill, I had accepted the role without pay, believing that with the Lord's help, the congregation would grow to the point where it could support my family and me financially. Sadly, it hadn't happened. Now, with a part-time job, I'd be spending fifteen hours a week less on my church work, and the hoped-for growth would be even less likely.

So from April until at least November of 1983, I suffered from another bout of depression. I questioned my calling to be a pastor, I was afraid to speak to outsiders about the Lord, and I didn't even pray much. I felt I'd failed as a church leader, and I no longer wanted to be one.

In reality, since we came to Naphill, several good things had happened, many with the help of invited evangelists and a children's mission in a tent on the village recreation ground. 47 children and adults had given their lives to Christ; five people had been healed; nine people had been baptized in water; and twelve children and five adults had been baptized in the Holy Spirit, including the mayoress of High Wycombe. One young man I led to Christ straight away spent three solid days in his bedroom reading the Bible, and he later became an effective street evangelist in London. No, my ministry to date hadn't been a tale of complete failure. Yet I *felt* that it had been.

Lamentably, during those months of depression, I sought comfort in entirely the wrong place: I started to write an ungodly multi-choice fantasy adventure book. I lost myself in a world of my creating, where I was the hero, welcomed by everyone I met, successfully overcoming every obstacle, and finally gaining my heart's desire! I knew what I was doing wasn't right, and I forced myself to destroy what I had written—only to start writing the same story again a few weeks later, this time bigger and better!

I developed an irritated colon, which disturbed my sleep and troubled me during the day. An investigation with what Don Double had once called a 'burial meal'[73] found nothing seriously wrong with me, but when the trouble got worse, I burnt the second book, and the irritation subsided. It had almost certainly been caused by self-induced stress.

In November, I gave in to an intensely strong temptation to write my book yet again! Because my time was now limited by working as a groundsman, it took me until March of the following year to complete what ended up as a seriously long book. Soon after finishing it, and filled with remorse once more, I burnt it again, and finally the temptation was broken.

Curiously, my December report to my family, friends, and trustees that year was optimistic, with news that the Sunday school attendance had risen to 35 and that we had a new Sunday school teacher. It described plans for a new way to run the Sunday morning services, with twenty minutes of all-age worship, followed by Sunday school teaching for the children, and for the adults, a lesson from a three-year course of foundational Christian doctrine that I had bought. The Sunday school teachers would do the same course with me on Tuesday evenings. I don't know if I was deceiving my readers or deceiving myself, but there was no mention of my depression.

It wasn't until many years later, in 2023, that I finally repented of that terrible dereliction of my responsibility as a pastor of Jesus Christ and I received the Lord's complete forgiveness. What troubled me most was not the content of the books, but the many hours that writing them had taken me away from my primary responsibility to the Lord to be a pastor to the flock he had entrusted to me.

---

[73] A barium meal.

❧ ❧ ❧ ❧ ❧ ❧ ❧

Early in 1984, Don Double got in touch with me. Miguel Pérez had organized a crusade for him in Osorno, to take place the following October. Don asked me if I would go there ten days beforehand to train counsellors and help to set things up. The Good News Crusade would pay all my expenses. It didn't take much thought for me to agree!

However, by June of that year, we were again running out of money. Fifteen hours a week of work on the pay of an assistant groundsman and a little additional income from the church had kept us afloat for more than a year, but it was not enough to support a family of six. At TRADA, I saw a notice advertising a vacancy for an engineer. With my degree in engineering, I thought it was worth applying, so, still wearing overalls and safety boots from my work building a wall, I entered the main building and knocked at the Chief Engineer's office door.

"Come in," said a kind voice.

Harold Burgess was a tall man with a deeply lined face, and he smelt of cigarette smoke.

"Good morning, sir," I began. (Best to be polite.) "I wanted to ask about the advertisement for an engineer."

"Oh yes?" He gave me an indulgent smile.

"I have a degree in mechanical engineering, and I've done a graduate apprenticeship. I don't know if that would qualify me for the post?"

"Oh, I see." No smile now. "Are you free? We could interview you now, if you like."

I was taken aback. "Well, I'm here."

"Wait a minute then while I fetch Mr Withers."

I'd assumed that I'd be given some notice of an interview, and I'd already been planning to hunt for my old university files and swat up some of the engineering I had learned, in case I was asked some testing questions. $M/I = E/R = p/y$, if I remembered rightly. Mr Burgess returned with his colleague.

"This is Mr Withers. He'll be leading the project. Won't you sit down?"

I found a chair and searched for somewhere near the desk to place it, between the heaps of papers and books on the floor.

"We have a research contract to investigate the use of timber in temporary works throughout the European Union. The contract will run for two years, and it will involve travelling to various European countries, visiting building sites and asking questions, involving 16 or 18 days of travel over the project's lifetime.

"Now, I know you are the minister of a church." (I had spoken to him once or twice in the canteen.) "Would your work as a minister preclude your travelling abroad, if necessary at weekends?"

This was extraordinary. "No, it wouldn't," I answered. "In January, the Lord told the church that I would be travelling in the future and that they must be prepared to release me for it!"

Mr Burgess exchanged a somewhat mystified look with John Withers. "So, would investigating temporary works interest you?"

"Yes, absolutely." (Anything to earn some money) "I can speak Spanish, French and a little German too."

An astonished smile now. "That's wonderful! What do you think, John?"

John Withers nodded. "I'd be happy to have Arnold work with me."

"All right." Harold Burgess turned to me. "Let me see if I can get in touch with the director. He's in Sheffield now, but I might be able to speak to him on the phone. Can you come back again in half an hour?"

Half an hour later, I was offered the job. No references, no certificates, no technical questions. The pay wasn't great, not even as much as I'd have earned as a Methodist minister. But it came with a generous pension scheme, and it would be sufficient for our needs in conjunction with my small income from the church. I was told there would be a rise after six months if my work proved satisfactory, so I was happy. I couldn't imagine how God had organised it all so perfectly again. I went home to tell Ann the good news.

"Do you know where the dictionary is?" I asked her. "I want to find out what temporary works are."

In time, I became Senior Engineer at the company. I helped design timber-frame houses, carried out various structural tests, and produced some twenty publications, including a foundational design manual published by the Institution of Structural Engineers for the design of timber buildings throughout Europe, which the manager of one company described as their 'Bible'. I wrote a widely-used suite of engineering design software, received a 'best speaker' award for one of many lectures I gave around the United Kingdom and the Republic of Ireland, and saved a new two-storey environmental school building in Dorset from probable collapse by identifying critical errors in its design by other engineers.

What I felt was particularly astounding was the timing of it all. If we'd left Chile a month or two later, the trustees would probably have already found someone else to lead the church in Naphill. Or if we'd left earlier, any talk about the forthcoming vacancy might not have begun. And if my sister had not seen the previous pastor walking into the church building just as she drove by... and if the research project hadn't cropped up just when it did... and I hadn't seen the advert for it... and... and...

God is amazing. Amazing! But then, of course, he is God. He is real. He can organize anything.

Chapter 28. Chile Re-visited, and a Spirit-led Drama

I started work as an engineer at TRADA in June 1984. Luis Palau, an Argentinian evangelist, was holding mass evangelistic meetings at the Queens Park Rangers football ground in London during June and the first half of July that summer. Despite my new full-time job and church responsibilities, I managed to organize six self-drive minibuses, three cars and one coach to take people to several of his meetings. I was even able to include some of my new fellow employees from TRADA on these trips, scaring the life out of them with my minibus driving, perhaps making them feel that they ought to get ready to meet God, just in case!

Of the people that we took to the meetings, nine were born again; eight Christians rededicated their lives to the Lord, and quite a few received counselling and ministry for other matters. As a result, we replaced our Sunday evening service with twenty minutes of praise and worship, followed by a 'nurture group' meeting, using a six-lesson course produced by Luis Palau's team. That part took about an hour and a half, and after that, we had an informal time of fellowship, either in someone's home or playing table tennis in the church hall.

Ann was encouraged by the progress of our older ladies whom she met each week: three of them bravely began to pray aloud in the meetings, and two of them asked for prayer to be filled with the Holy Spirit. A third lady in her eighties was even seen dancing during the time of praise on Easter Sunday evening.

Susan Bickerstaffe had confessed to a fear of heights. I prayed with her, and the Lord answered our prayers: two weeks later, she went on a big wheel with her husband Ian at a fun fair. Her only previous attempt had ended in panic. This time she enjoyed it so much, especially when it unexpectedly stopped with them at the top, that she wanted another go! They also went for walks along the North Devon cliff tops, and she stood at the very edges to admire the view while Ian wished we had not prayed quite so hard!

❧ ❧ ❧ ❧ ❧ ❧ ❧

On Monday, October 8th, 1984, in response to Don Double's invitation, I set off for my beloved Chile once more to prepare for Don's and Mike's upcoming evangelistic crusades.

My principal job was to train evangelistic counsellors for a major crusade which had been organised by Miguel Perez in the city of Osorno. Don had kept his promise to Miguel. But my first stop wasn't for crusade work—it was to visit Bío-Bío University, a university specializing in timber structures in the city of Concepción. I had already learned enough at TRADA to discuss possible collaboration between the two organizations. Chile has vast softwood timber resources, and TRADA specialized in grading timber for structural use. At the university, I got to know several of the senior staff.

Next, I spent two days with Miguel and the church leaders and counsellors in Osorno, then went on to Punta Arenas, where I had a long conversation about Chilean timber with a mechanical engineer named Rodrigo. A French commission had reported that, properly developed, the Chilean timber industry could provide more income than copper, and he told me that several foreign firms had expressed an interest in developing the sector, in cooperation with Chilean labour and technology.

Two Swedish missionaries I knew invited me to a fondue meal in the evening, and at about 9:30 p.m. I asked if people in their Assembly of God church had prophecies or visions. This was just what they wanted to talk about, and I spent the next two hours teaching on prophecy in the church. The following morning, I spent another hour talking to the wife of the new headmaster of the British School about the character of a prophet, prophetic motivation and prophetic preparation. I never realized that I knew so much! I came alive in Chile.

Don and Mike duly arrived in Osorno for four nights of evangelistic meetings, after which we flew back to the capital for a final evangelistic meeting in Santiago. Here, something remarkable took place.

Mike was planning to teach on Psalm 107:19,20: *'They cried to the Lord in their trouble, and he delivered them from their distress; he sent forth his word and healed them, and delivered them from destruction.'*

The point Mike wanted to make that evening was that Jesus has set us free from bondage to sin and death, but for this to be a reality, we have to believe it: we have to act on it and leave behind our former way of life, and walk into the life of freedom that he has obtained for us.

"Arnold," he said before the meeting. "Do you fancy doing a bit of acting?"

"Yes, I like acting!"

"There you are," said Don. "I told you he'd say yes."

"What do you want me to do?" I asked.

"While I'm speaking, could you act the part of a man sitting in jail, thinking that he is about to be executed for his crimes? He's scared, but then the jail door will open, and someone will tell him that he has been pardoned. But when you hear this, instead of jumping up with joy, you turn away, unable to believe what you have heard. Instead of walking out into freedom, you remain trapped and terrified in the cell. What do you think?"

"Yes, I can do that, but can we make it more dramatic? Let's say that his execution day is a Saturday, and he is thrown into jail five days earlier. Tell the story with the man getting more dejected and more terrified every day, and I will mime the part as you do this, counting off on my fingers the days to my execution. Five more days, and that's it; only four more days and my life will end; three more days now, and so on. Can we do that?"

We did. Each day in Mike's story, I became more dejected, more despairing, and more terrified, until on the last day, the fifth day, when I was told I was free to go, I so refused to believe it that I put my hands over my ears.

We rehearsed it once and performed it live at the evening meeting. When I sat down, Don whispered to me, "That was prophetic!" And it was. For this is what we learned afterwards...

The evangelistic meeting took place on a Saturday evening, and on the previous Tuesday, (five days earlier), two young brothers named Felipe and Francesco did something extremely foolish. They were caught trying to steal two guns from the back of a police car. It was still during the military dictatorship of General Pinochet, when trying to steal a gun from a police car was about the stupidest thing anyone could do, apart from being caught! And they *were* caught, and they were thrown into jail.

Because of their young age, their mother was told what had happened. She went to see them and gave a Bible to them, telling them to read it and amend their foolish ways. One of them began to read it, but his brother refused, blaming God for letting them get into trouble! As each day passed, the two young men became more discouraged, more depressed, and more fearful. They had no idea what their fate would be. The Bible-reading brother told God he was sorry, and he prayed for their release.

And then Saturday arrived, the Saturday on which our evangelistic meeting was due to take place. That same day, in the morning, after five days in prison, they were both told that they had been granted a provisional pardon: they were free to go but must never try such a thing again, or they would be in real trouble. Perhaps, like the man in Mike's story, they too couldn't believe it at first.

As soon as they got home, their mother insisted that they come to the meeting in the evening to thank God for answering her prayers for their release. You can imagine how they felt as they listened to Mike's teaching and watched my acting. It was as though God had been watching what had been happening to them all the week, and he was now acting it out in front of their eyes!

When Don invited people to come to the front of the church in repentance and commit their lives to Christ, Felipe and Francisco were the first to jump up and rush to the front. Furthermore, one of them was also filled with the Holy Spirit and began praising God in tongues!

As a result of our little play and their consequent repentance, two young men were saved not from earthly imprisonment but from God's final judgment and condemnation, and they received a free pardon for all their sins that would last them for eternity!

Chapter 29. Hints of a New Ministry

On returning to England, I suggested that TRADA assist the Chilean forestry industry in grading their timber so that it could be sold in Europe. This was developed into a firm proposal, which we submitted to the Chilean authorities. If accepted, it would lead to thousands of pounds worth of work for TRADA and many millions of pounds worth of income for Chile. The new head of engineering and I visited the Chilean embassy in London to talk to the Trade Secretary about it.

As a result of these contacts, TRADA was invited to participate in two conferences in Chile in 1986, one on timber bridges to withstand earthquakes, and the other on timber engineering in general. As God's appointed key, I was opening yet more doors!

❧ ❧ ❧ ❧ ❧ ❧ ❧

In the autumn of 1986, Don Double once again enlisted my services to go before him and Mike Darwood to Chile, to prepare the way for crusades in three different cities. I was to train evangelistic counsellors, to teach on church life, and to give newspaper and television interviews as pre-crusade publicity. And I arranged another visit to Bío-Bío University.

This time, my visit was to last three and a half weeks, starting on September 22nd 1986, and my dear wife Ann was to accompany me. Somehow, I'd found the money to pay half her fare, and Don's GNC organization agreed to pay the other half. My mother must have come to look after the children while we were away.

The itinerary was even more complex than before, and it included some crucial meetings at Bío-Bío University, which were later to have a part in the Lord's slowly unfolding purpose for my life.

Before we left, I attended a commissioning service in which people prayed for our travels and our forthcoming ministry in Chile. A prophetic man named Dennis Ball prayed for Don, Mike and me, and the Lord gave him these words: "You will speak to rulers and governors, and some of your dreams will be fulfilled." I felt this was so significant that I wrote out all the words I could find in the Psalms about rulers and how God wanted rulers to rule.

≈ ≈ ≈ ≈ ≈ ≈ ≈

Every time I visited Chile I was reminded of how much I loved the country and I wanted to return. So during some free time at a timber conference at Bío-Bío University, I chatted with Carlos Ilabaca, one of the organizers.

"Carlos, what do you think about the possibility of my coming here as a lecturer? I mean, on the staff, perhaps part-time."

"It's not out of the question. But you wouldn't be paid as much as in England."

"What kind of salaries do lecturers in Chile earn?"

We talked about it a bit more. So far as I could gather, the overall cost of living in that part of Chile was somewhat less than in England. Fruit, vegetables, and milk were cheaper, for the region had a Mediterranean climate, and not much further south there was extensive dairy farming. Gas and electricity were perhaps a little more expensive, but it was never particularly cold in the winter, so perhaps that wouldn't matter. Imported goods were more expensive.

Our conversation made me think.

≈ ≈ ≈ ≈ ≈ ≈ ≈

Ann and I spent the night with Bishop Ian Morrison, his wife Marion, and their Great Aunt Teddy who lived with them and was about to celebrate her 100th birthday.

I asked Ian that evening, "What do you think about the possibility of Ann getting a job teaching English in Concepción?"

"It's not out of the question. Saint John's College was established by the British Council years ago and is bilingual. They sometimes struggle to find English teachers of English rather than American ones. Are you both thinking of coming back here then?"

"I don't know. It's an idea floating in my mind."

"I would like to come," said Ann.

"If you do come here, we'd love to have you both in our church!"

That night I had a most vivid dream. I dreamt that someone gave me a lot of money in three cheques totalling £1.2 million, two of £500,000 and one of £200,000. It brought to mind Dennis Ball's prophecy: "And some of your dreams will be fulfilled."

The following week, we visited people in three different towns. In Temuco, I heard about a man who had become a believer in Jesus. He then completed a Bible course that led to a diploma to teach in the church. He made a living selling fish, but the very day his diploma came, he was arrested because he couldn't produce his licence, which allowed him to sell food on the street. He had left the licence at home, but the arresting officer didn't believe him.

The man had a family, and they lived from day to day on whatever he could sell that day, but now he couldn't sell anything because he was in jail. He was torn between praying for rescue and losing faith in God altogether, for his imprisonment almost seemed to him like a punishment of some kind.

However, the next day, a letter from a Baptist church in the USA arrived at his local church. It contained an unexpected and unsolicited gift for 'a family in need'. The cheque was cashed, and the money was taken to the man's family. Someone from the church visited him and told him the good news. Two days later, he was released, rejoicing in God's goodness, and stronger than ever in his faith.

Next, in a brief visit to Puerto Montt two days after this, someone told me how hard it was to evangelize the poorest people. "We go with the good news of a life to come, but the communists take them food and clothing for life here and now, so they choose communism rather than Christianity." I realized how important it was for the church to have the means to help people materially as well as spiritually.

Then there was a partly finished building in Punta Arenas, close to the Methodist Church. Pillars of spiralling steel rebar sprouted out of the concrete slab, waiting to be encased in concrete that never came. I asked about the building. I was told that a Yugoslavian church had started to build it two years earlier to be a youth centre, but their money had run out.

So, for the third time in a week, I saw how the church's ministry—in Chile at least—was being limited by a lack of money, but was blessed when people from a more wealthy country provided it. And I recalled my dream in Concepción about money. Was the Lord saying something to me? "And some of your dreams will be fulfilled," Dennis Ball had said.

Years ago, I completed several questionnaires on spiritual gifts. The three top gifts that always came up for me were teacher, missionary and financial giver. I could understand the first two, but the problem with giving was that while I did enjoy providing money to help people, I never seemed to have much of it to give them. Yet now, the Lord appeared to have given me a dream in which I would receive a vast amount of money. Was he planning on giving me some new ministry involving what was apparently one of my three major spiritual gifts? And what did that have to do with my growing desire to return to Chile?

Chapter 30. Miracles of Healing, Prayer in the Spirit and a Reluctant Recall

The Osorno pastors had invited some local dignitaries to an afternoon tea, doubtless hoping that they would attend the evangelistic event the following week. Among the people invited were the mayor of Osorno and Pinnochet's regional governor, a tall and important man who arrived in his military uniform. Unfortunately, the mayor had a cold and couldn't attend, so I was given his seat, right next to the regional governor! "You will speak to rulers and governors," Dennis had said. So I took out my prepared teaching and asked the Governor if he would accept and read it. "Seguramente," he assured me. "Assuredly. Thank you." He folded it up neatly and placed it in the breast pocket of his uniform.

🌿 🌿 🌿 🌿 🌿 🌿 🌿

Between the preparatory visits to Osorno and Punta Arenas, Ann and I briefly visited Miguel Perez and his family in Coyhaique, midway between the two cities. Coyhaique is a lovely little town, entirely surrounded by mountains and with no easy access to the mainland other than by air. Miguel's church denomination had sent him there, with Ana and their three small children, to start a new work. They lived in a tiny wooden house with so little income that I couldn't imagine how they got by. Someone had offered to give them a truckload of topsoil so that they could grow some vegetables, but the contractor had tipped it out so close to their front door that it was challenging to get in and out of the house!

On Sunday night, I preached in Miguel's church, which was hardly big enough to hold the congregation of 100 who had nearly all joined during the two years that he and Ana had been there. The service lasted three hours. Ann had two words of knowledge, which resulted in one woman being delivered from depression and another being healed of heart trouble after suffering from it for forty years. We met them again at the crusade a week later, and they were both bouncing with life.

The Coyhaique crusade the following week lasted four nights, and thanks to Miguel's unique organizational abilities, between 2000 and 3000 people attended each night. On the first two nights, the meetings were broadcast on the radio. After the first of these, I asked the radio station's owner about the listeners' reactions.

"I think people liked it," he replied. "But many of us think that when we get to heaven, we shall find that all religions are similar."

I reported this to Don. He immediately changed his chosen Bible verse for the following evening's preaching to Jesus's words in John 14:6. "No religion can get you to heaven!" he proclaimed. "Jesus said, 'I am the way, the truth and the life. No one comes to the Father but by me.' Jesus said anyone who tries to enter heaven any other way is a thief. I want to tell you tonight that heaven is thief-proof!"

The radio man was so absorbed in Don's message that he broadcast it for 35 minutes more than we had paid for, commentating enthusiastically on people's response in the stadium to the appeal for people to commit their lives to Jesus as Lord, and completely wiping out the programme that was scheduled to follow!

At the end of all Don and Mike's crusade meetings, people in need of healing queued up for prayer. They did that because Don and Mike told them that Jesus could heal today, just as he did when he walked on the earth. And he can, and he does. On the final night, ten of us prayed for the sick for one and a half hours!

One little girl who'd had a cleft palate spoke plainly for the first time—she said "Papa!" through the microphone. A young man testified to being healed of a hernia; a girl who'd not been able to walk properly, jumped safely off the platform; a woman's twisted mouth and partly paralysed face were restored.

Some of the clinical needs people expressed in the Coyhaique crusade were beyond my limited Spanish, and since I always find it hard to hear what people are saying when there is a lot of noise around me, I sometimes struggled a bit. Ann and I were praying for a queue of supplicants one night when a lady asked us to pray for her son. She mentioned a word that sounded like 'testicle,' but I wasn't at all sure whether I had got it right. I didn't want to get into an embarrassing and hard-to-understand conversation by asking for more information, so I prayed for her son in Spanish as best I could, hoping I hadn't completely misunderstood her.

Sometimes, misunderstandings due to language can be comical. Peter Gammons, one of Don's young associate evangelists, was once preaching in Norfolk. An old gentleman asked Peter to pray for his feet.

"What's the matter with your feet?" Peter asked.

"They've got screws in 'em," the man explained.

"Screws?! So what do you want me to do for you?"

"Get 'em out, boy. Ask the good Lord to get 'em out."

Feeling a complete fool, Peter went ahead. He knelt down and placed his hands on the gentleman's feet. "Screws, in the name of Jesus Christ, come out!"

It was only afterwards that someone explained to Peter that 'screws' was Norfolkese for rheumatism!

The following day in Coyhaique, I went out for a walk. I was looking up at a flock of eagles circling above me when a grubby little boy approached, holding out his hand. I thought he wanted me to give him a peso, but no—he wanted to shake my hand. He was the boy whose mother had asked us to pray for the previous evening. He told me he had been due to go into hospital for an operation on a testicle.

"Jesus has healed me!" he said with a radiant smile!

At the close of the meeting on the second evening, Don asked me to bring it to an end in prayer. When he and Mike spoke, they spoke in English, and Ian Morrison stood at their side, interpreting what they said into Spanish. But Ian didn't stand up with me when I got up to pray. I was expected to pray directly in my not-entirely-fluent Spanish, in front of an audience of some 2500 people in the stadium and a radio audience of unknown numbers.

Oh well, here goes, I thought. *I only wish I were not so compliant. Anyone else would have asked for Ian's help.*

After my first few sentences, there were one or two polite 'Amens' from the audience, but it wasn't going too well. I had to think first what to say and then how to say it in Spanish. It was like trying to ignite a sparkler. I looked to the Lord for inspiration and began praying as his Spirit led me. I started to pray more freely, and the 'Amens' increased in volume. I focused on the Lord to whom I was speaking rather than on what I was saying. Then I noticed with mild alarm that some of the words I was saying—presumably still in Spanish—were words that I didn't know. But the more I let go and the more I let God's Spirit speak through me—whether I knew all the words or not—the louder the 'Amens' and 'Aleluyas' sounded. My own final 'Amen' was thunderously echoed back all around the stadium.

I sat down, and Don turned to me. "Why can't you pray like that in English?" he demanded.

212 people were counselled during the Coyhaique crusade, 80% for salvation. The greatest miracle of all is when a person who is spiritually dead is born again and begins everlasting life!

🌿 🌿 🌿 🌿 🌿 🌿 🌿

The next stop was my beloved Punta Arenas, the city at the end of the earth. This time, the four days of crusade meetings were held in a gymnasium. Once more, the Lord demonstrated his love and power through many beautiful miracles. And what was still more important was that some 600 people began a new life with Jesus at its centre.

Many of the city's leading business and professional people paid £5 each to have breakfast on the Saturday morning at the Cape Horn Hotel, to meet Don Double and listen to him talk about 'True Success'. They were amazed to learn how God filled Don with the Holy Spirit as a 20-year-old unable to read or write and turned him into an international Christian leader, evangelist, teacher and author, ministering in some thirty different nations worldwide. When the moment came to invite these men and women to receive Jesus Christ as the lord of their life, business and home, almost every one of them raised their hand without hesitation.

During the ministry that week, I was especially blessed by receiving several words of knowledge, through which the Lord supernaturally showed me the causes of some people's problems. This was something that hadn't happened to me before. Throughout the three and a half weeks in Chile, whenever I opened my mouth to pray, I was anointed with God's power in a way that never occurred in England.

The fruit of that crusade in Punta Arenas was even greater than that of the one I had organized when we lived there.

The final meeting was on follow-up, teaching people how to live as disciples of Jesus. People were counselled and prayed for. The Lord removed a mental blockage in Ann over Spanish, and he touched her heart to heal the hurts she had suffered from misunderstandings and rejection, both when we lived in Chile and in England. She began to weep, and she didn't stop weeping for two hours as the Saviour washed away all those past hurts. The Lord gave her such a love for Chile that she couldn't wait to go there again! In the first few weeks following our return to England, Ann was free of the headaches and indigestion that had troubled her since we moved to Naphill.

❧ ❧ ❧ ❧ ❧ ❧ ❧

On the plane back to England, Don left his seat at the front of the cabin where he and Mike always tried to sit because the seats there had more legroom, and he squeezed himself in next to me.

"Mike and I believe that Chile is where you should be," he told me. "Ian said the same thing. You are a different person in Chile, and it's clear that your anointing is for there rather than England. So isn't there a way that you and Ann could raise the money to return there? What do you think?"

I didn't know what to say. How could we do that?

On our return home, I talked it over with Ann.

"What do you think about it, my love?" I asked.

My wife looked straight at me with a solemn expression on her face. I knew that expression: it always presaged a significant statement.

"I believe God wants us to go back," she said.

I trusted my wife on matters of revelation. But leaving any of our children behind in England would be hard. So very, very hard. It would also be hard to be separated from our two widowed mothers and my sisters and their children.

I talked to the Lord about it. He reminded me of past words he had given: the word given to me at Richmond College—*"Am I a God at hand, says the Lord, and not a God far off?"*; the word given at my baptism—*"It is the Lord who goes before you; he will be with you, he will not fail you or forsake you; do not fear or be dismayed"*; and the momentous words from Isaiah chapter 49 on the day he called us to Chile, including the end of verse six—*"I will give you as a light to the nations, that my salvation may reach to the end of the earth."*

How could I be a light anywhere in Chile if we stayed in England? Did those words from the Bible still apply? After nine years of waiting, we had lived in Chile for such a short time. And the very week that we returned home, the Chilean government had granted us permanent residence there. That couldn't have been a coincidence, surely? Yet I shrank from leaving the apparent security of life in Buckinghamshire.

God's Spirit led me to Mark 10:29–30:

Jesus said, "Truly, I say to you, there is no one who has left house or brothers or sisters or mother or father or children, or lands, for my sake and for the gospel, who will not receive a hundredfold now in this time, houses and brothers and sisters, and mothers and children and lands, with persecutions, and in the age to come eternal life."

Then the Spirit led my thoughts to the great Passover feast, which Jesus said he was looking forward to celebrating with his disciples when he returned to the earth to reign:[74] *"Many will come from East and West and sit at table with Abraham, Isaac, and Jacob in the kingdom of heaven,"* he said.[75] And I thought, "How could I sit there next to people such as Saint Paul, John Wesley or Mother Theresa, or next to Christians who have been martyred for upholding the Bible and preaching the gospel—how could I greet them without embarrassment and shame if I had knowingly rejected a call from God to take his great news of everlasting salvation to the people of Chile again, preferring instead the comfort and ease and security of a nice job, a nice house, a nice education for my children, a nice pension, and a nice retirement in this nice country of England?

And to seal the matter, when I asked the children what they thought, they supported the idea!

"I'd quite like you to go," said Julian. In any case, he was hoping to leave the nest the following September to begin a year's paid industrial sponsorship before he entered university.

"I think you'll be very happy in Chile," Emerald said. "I won't mind if you go there."

"I'd love to go back to Chile," Joseph said.

"So would I," said Zachary.

But how could I raise the money to return?

---

[74] Luke 22:15–18
[75] Matthew 8:11

195

Chapter 31. Saved from Death, and an Astonishing Offer of Help

On the morning of November 13th, 1986, I woke up with the distinct impression that the Lord was going to speak to me about money through a passage in a Christian magazine that I was reading through. Sure enough, I read John 4:36: *"He who reaps receives wages, and gathers fruit for eternal life, so that sower and reaper may rejoice together."* I had a sudden conviction that something special was going to happen that day.

"Today is money day!" I declared as I got out of bed.

Before I left for work, a letter arrived in the post, offering me a post at the Building Research Establishment near Watford on a salary of £11,000 a year, which was more than I earned at TRADA. When I told TRADA's director that day, he offered to match the salary if I would stay. I readily agreed, since I wouldn't have to travel to Watford daily.

That same evening, I visited my friends Gos and Diana Home. Gos told me about his plans to set up a company to be known as the Christian Resources Exhibition, and he asked me if I would be interested in joining him as its first administrator.[76] But I believed I would soon return to Chile, so I felt it was wrong to accept his invitation, even though the pay would undoubtedly have been generous.

Being effectively offered three jobs in one day was a kind of miracle. Through that, and increasing my salary without my

---

[76] Gospatrick Home did set up the Christian Resources Exhibitions. It became the UK's major exhibition for Christian organisations, churches and suppliers to churches and individual Christians, exhibiting twice a year. The exhibition continues to this day.

having to ask, the Lord seemed to be telling me that he could provide me with the money I needed.

However, before we could do much about Don's suggestion, Ann became unwell again. She started having psychotic thoughts and became more and more withdrawn, until finally she stopped speaking altogether. My precious wife had to return to hospital.

This time, the hospital was a dedicated mental hospital in Stone, not far from Stoke Mandeville in Buckinghamshire. Three or four weeks after Ann was admitted, I was woken up in the night by a telephone call.

"Mr. Page? I'm calling from St John's Hospital. I'm sorry to call you like this, but your wife's condition is extremely serious. She'd having breathing problems and severe heart palpitations. It's possible she may not survive until the morning. I'm so sorry. Would you like to come here now, to be with her, in case...?"

I thought for a moment. Zachary, our youngest, was then nine years old, but I was still concerned about leaving him and the other children in the house at night without me.

"Can you give me five minutes, and I'll call you back?" I asked. I needed time to think.

"Yes, of course. Let me give you my direct number."

I wrote down the phone number and rang off.

What should I do? What should I do? I needed the Lord to keep me calm: I needed the Lord to guide me.

"Tell me what to do, Lord."

I remembered a time when Joseph was five or six years old. We were waiting to cross a road in snowy weather, and I was holding his hand.

He asked, "Are you very strong, Daddy?"

"Yes, I am fairly strong. Stronger than you, at any rate. Why do you ask?"

"Because I always feel safe when I am holding your hand," he said.

At that moment I knew God was with me as always, holding my hand. There was no need to feel frightened.

Just as I'd done years earlier when Ann had her post-natal depression, I turned to the Psalms to see if the Lord would say something to me through them. I opened my Bible, which was always at our bedside. I found the book of Psalms and read the first two verses that I saw:

The Lord God is a sun and shield; he bestows favour and honour.
No good thing does the Lord withhold from those who walk
uprightly. O Lord of hosts, blessed is the man who trusts in thee!
Psalm 84:11,12

Ann is a good thing, I thought. I don't believe the Lord will take her away from me. I'm going to trust him in this, just as it says. Perhaps it didn't make sense, given the nurse's urgent words, but I had peace about it. I phoned the hospital.

"Thank you for calling me, but I won't come now. I'll call again in the morning to see how she is."

I thanked the Lord for his words of assurance, prayed that Ann would survive and recover, and went back to sleep.

I called the hospital at 7:00 a.m.

"Hello, Mr Page," the nurse replied. "I have good news for you. The emergency seems to be over. We think your wife was allergic to a drug we had been using.[77] She's still not well, but you can visit her this afternoon if you'd like to."

I don't recall exactly how long Ann had to remain in hospital, but it was several months before she was back to normal.

Ann's illness delayed following up Don's suggestion about returning to Chile, but in May 1987 I made a start, beginning one of the most astonishing twelve months of my life. Was it God's unfolding of an amazing and wholly unexpected plan, or

---

[77] Imiprimine

did I somehow make the biggest, most terrible mistake of my life? I sometimes wonder, even now, if I got it right.

🌿 🌿 🌿 🌿 🌿 🌿 🌿

The Holy Spirit had laid on my heart Chile's second city, Concepción. It was there that the Lord gave me that vivid dream about the £1.2 million, and it was there that I had built up a strong relationship with the staff at the university. I'd stayed there with Bishop Ian Morrison and his wife Marion, so we already had some association with the Anglican church in the city. Santiago, which I had never felt drawn to, had many large churches, and I could see no reason why this city, too, should not host such churches for the glory of God.

Thus it was that early in May 1987, I wrote out a 19-stage costed plan to establish not a church, but a Christian city! I planned to do this in collaboration with other church pastors there, in particular with the help of my friend and Christian brother, Miguel Pérez. In Coyhaique, Miguel had established a congregation of a 100 people in two years, so my plan began on the reasonable assumption that Miguel and I together could start by doing the same thing in Concepción—but with four of us including our wives, instead of just Miguel and Ana. I hoped this could be followed by an annual increase of 40% in the number of people with us.[78] I thought this was not an unreasonable goal, especially with an evangelist and administrator like Miguel on the job, and with all the discipleship teaching material I had written when I lived in Chile.

I worked out that if we could begin with twelve of us and maintain such a rate of increase with the help and blessing of the Holy Spirit, then after 25 years there would be over 50,000 new disciples in Concepción.

---

[78] If a church has ten members and four new people join it within a year, its membership has increased by 40%.

Multiplication works when every new believer, or almost every new believer, becomes an evangelist and creates new believers in turn. Bishop Vásquez at the Jotabeche Church said that every one of his church's 350,000 members was an evangelist. Evangelism is not the job of a pastor. It's the sheep that have the baby sheep, not the shepherd. And for every new believer to be an evangelist, every new believer needs to be taught and helped to do this, which is one thing I planned to do. It would be easy to translate my two little booklets into Spanish.

I wrote to Miguel about it, and he promptly replied. Yes, he'd be pleased to work with me as I had suggested. Don Double had been talking to him about a crusade in that selfsame city in 1988, and Miguel was already beginning to plan for it there. So he would know all the pastors and the needs and opportunities in the city. Amazing!

❧ ❧ ❧ ❧ ❧ ❧ ❧

For some reason that I don't recall now, I told the Lord that I would knock on three metaphorical doors in search of initial financial support for me and my family: the UK Assemblies of God, the Evangelical Union of South America, and the University of Bío-Bío in Concepción.

Apart from the Methodist Church, the Christian denomination I'd had the most to do with in Chile was the Assemblies of God, and two of our closest friends in Chile were AoG pastors. So I wrote a letter to the AoG's Overseas Missions Chairman in the UK. I explained my vision for Concepción to him and asked if it would be possible for the AoG to help us get there. A warm and generous man, Ray Belfield replied to my letter in a remarkably positive way, inviting Ann and me to meet him, which we did, still in the month of May. Despite Ann's recent illness, she was fully committed to our return to Chile and was well enough to attend the interview.

Amazingly—since Ray knew nothing about us except what we told him, and we were not even members of his denomination—he gave me the authority to visit AoG churches in Britain to share our vision and to invite each church or the individuals in it to commit to regular ongoing financial support and prayer for our mission to Chile.

"You need to get on with this project while you still have some colour in your hair," Ray said. "You're not a youngster anymore. You'll probably need something like £12,000 a year, and raising that amount will take at least 18 months. If we're going to support you, I'd like you to minister in an AoG church in England for 18 months while you are fundraising. You should buy a house near an AoG church and get in touch now with someone in the AoG in Chile to start having conversations with them. You'll need their covering over your ministry."

How does one buy a house with next to no money in the bank? How can I minister in an AoG church while the house I am living in requires me to pastor Naphill Evangelical Church?

As I mentioned earlier, one of my many faults is being too compliant. Was it a mistake to accept what Ray said without questioning him about its practicalities? Or was I merely doing what I had told the congregation in Aylsham to do in my first sermon as a Methodist minister—to walk by faith, not by sight? Perhaps someone would give us a house!

Chapter 32. Chile for Christ!

Even though the AoG church had flung open their door to me, I decided I would still knock on the other two doors as well.

A spokesperson for the Evangelical Union of South America answered my metaphorical knock in a friendly manner, but he didn't open the door. Chile would be a new country for them, he said, so we agreed to put my application on ice.

I didn't have to knock on the third door: it was open already. Several of the senior staff from the University of Bío-Bío had visited TRADA during the previous two years, and one in particular had urged me to apply for a job at the university. Our two organisations did similar work, and TRADA was currently negotiating a contract to help the university in Concepción to develop the use of timber in construction throughout Chile. It was part of the project I had initiated three years earlier.

Several people advised me to accept this invitation, suggesting that I work half-time at the university. Working there would give me helpful insight into how Chileans lived and provide contacts with people in the academic, building, timber and student sectors of society. In August, a minister at a Good News Crusade family camp in Malvern that we attended advised me to combine secular work with church work as a 'living epistle'.

I was now totally committed to returning to Chile, as was Ann. We each had a mind and spirit of our own, yet we were always in agreement in matters related to God—what a blessing that was in our marriage!

🌿 🌿 🌿 🌿 🌿 🌿 🌿

Jesus said, *"If anyone comes to me and does not hate his own father and mother and wife and children and brothers and sisters, yes, and even his own life, he cannot be my disciple.'*[79] So we believed that whatever Jesus wanted us to do had to come first. But the question was this: was it really what Jesus wanted us to do? Or was my desire to build a Christian city actually a desire to make a name for myself?

I talked to my church members about it. The church had grown again, despite my full-time work at TRADA. The members unreservedly supported our plan, believing the way would open up for us if it were God's will. In that case, they believed he would provide an able pastor to take my place among them, too.

[Prayer and Newsletter No. 22, July 1987]

> *Our friends Miguel and Ana Pérez in Coyhaique have had a difficult time this year. Miguel has suffered from health problems— I believe because of overwork and poor diet—and he's had financial difficulties due to the resulting medical bills. The construction of the new church building has come to a halt due to a lack of money, yet people continue to be saved, and the church grows.*

In August, Miguel Pérez spoke about my plans to some other pastors in his church's denomination. They told him that they had been asking the Lord for several years to help them start a work in Concepción, and they believed that this was God's answer to their prayers. They promised us all the spiritual, legal and pastoral help they could give us.

With that final reassurance, I went ahead and wrote a letter of application to Bío-Bío University for a part-time lecturer position. I contacted St John's School and was told there might be an opening for Ann to teach there, but we should ask again when we were ready to move to Chile. And as advised, I wrote to Victor Paredes, the General Secretary of the AoG in Chile,

---

[79] Luke 14:26

seeking his agreement to my ministry as an AoG missionary there.

Miguel visited Concepción in September and was amazed to find a church building with a small flat above it for sale in the heart of the city. He said it would be a 'fabulous place' to begin our ministry. Its present congregation had outgrown it, and Miguel was investigating its cost. Furthermore, a Chilean pastor about to retire wrote to me to say that he was 'at my service'. Other pastors in Chile and England offered us the support of their churches.

I then received a letter from Bío-Bío University, formally offering me a contract to work two days a week from August 1988 for a salary of £1500 per annum.

The problem of raising the rest of the money we needed might loom over us like the Paine Towers, but Jesus said that any mountain can be disposed of by faith in God. And it seemed to me that God could not have made it any clearer that this particular mountain-problem was destined for demolition.

It was time to start fund raising!

✿ ✿ ✿ ✿ ✿ ✿ ✿

I aimed to raise £20,000 per annum through promises of regular support by visiting churches around Great Britain and sharing the vision that the Lord had given me. Ray—that encouraging AoG Overseas Missions Chairman—had said we would need £12,000 per annum. However, I thought we would need £8000 more than this: £2500 per annum towards our children's accommodation with friends in England and for their summer holiday flights to Chile and back; £4500 per annum to pay for a twenty-year mortgage on a house purchase for rental in England; and £1000 for our accommodation in Chile, supplemented from renting our new house in England, at least until a growing church in Chile could support us.[80]

So, on October 31st 1987, I set out a fund raising plan.

---

[80] All 1987 prices

❧ ❧ ❧ ❧ ❧ ❧ ❧

The usual way to make a fundraising visit to a church is to offer to preach there on Sunday, combining an explanation of the ministry and its need for support with a faith-building message for the congregation, perhaps followed by prayer ministry to any needy people. Such visits, particularly to larger churches, might easily raise more than £10 per month.

However, I was still responsible to the trustees for conducting Sunday worship in the church at Naphill. Any visits I made would have to be to existing weeknight evenings when attendance is usually far smaller than on Sundays. I couldn't see people wanting to come out to a special meeting to listen to someone they'd never heard of ask them for money. Even if each visit produced promises of support totalling £10 per month, I'd have to make 167 such visits for my annual income to reach £20,000. At two visits a week, that would take nearly two years. It would be hard.

The only practical solution I could see was to resign my appointment at Naphill Evangelical Church. Then I could visit AoG churches on Sundays as a visiting preacher, which was what Ray had advised me to do. But if I resigned, where would we live? Did the Lord want us to trust him to provide a house for us? Looking back, I think we should have asked him if he wanted to do that. But we didn't ask him. So far as I recall, the idea never occurred to us. Was that a failure of vision? Was it a failure of faith? Did we miss the Lord's first choice for us and take another pathway leading to his second choice instead? Or did the Lord purposely not suggest the idea to us because it wasn't what he wanted us to do?

I went ahead with my attempts at fund raising without resigning from the church.

❧ ❧ ❧ ❧ ❧ ❧ ❧

I created some headed notepaper, copying the iconic style of the word 'Chile' used on publications by the Chilean government, and printing a silhouette of Chile down the left-hand side. Along the bottom were the words of our initial call in Isaiah 49:6: *"I will give you as a light to the nations, that my salvation may reach to the ends of the earth."*.

And by faith, I opened a 'Chile for Christ' bank account.

Printed on the new headed paper, I sent a letter to every Christian and church I knew, explaining in outline what I was going to do, how God had called me to do it, how the Assemblies of God would be supporting us, and how I wanted to visit as many churches as possible during the coming months to share the vision and invite individuals and churches to support us financially and by prayer. I asked those who read the letter if I could visit their church to talk about Chile for Christ.

My new ministry had been launched!

I managed to book a meeting in Aylsham before Christmas. Two people agreed to set up a monthly standing order, and two family members did the same. We had our first four sponsors.

And after that, everything began to unravel.

Chapter 33. God Reveals His Perfect Plan

I managed to speak at only two further promotional meetings, and neither of them produced any additional money. In February, I met a Christian pensions consultant to discuss transferring my company pension to a private one in anticipation of leaving TRADA. He said it was essential for me to have adequate insurance cover for Ann and to buy a house, since the house we lived in went with the Naphill church. If I were to die, Ann and the children would have nowhere to live. But I still couldn't see how we could ever buy a house.

The Bible says that with God nothing will be impossible, but was it possible that in this matter I was not with God? It was looking increasingly difficult to raise what we needed to support ourselves in Chile, let alone a Chilean pastor and his wife as well.

I decided to attend a prayer meeting on the first Saturday morning in March. A local Anglican Church had organised it as part of a day of prayer for the nation. Near the end of the meeting, people were invited to share any revelations God had given to them. One lady said she had seen a beautiful rose bush, which turned brown and died and was cut down. She believed that God was speaking about something that had to be cut down out of someone's life, something that might be very precious and very big, but it had to die. As she watched, she saw a circle of new rose bushes, none yet in bloom, surrounding where the first rose had been. The bushes intertwined with each other like a great crown of thorns. Then they all began to bloom together.

As she shared this vision, I became suddenly alert. I wondered whether the Lord was speaking to me, saying that we were not, after all, to go to Concepción. The words 'very precious and very big' seemed particularly applicable. I looked around at the other people in the meeting: it didn't appear that the revelation was meaningful to anyone else. But what did the circle of new rose bushes signify?

Before our Sunday morning service the following day, Barbara, our church treasurer, spoke to me.

"How did yesterday's prayer meeting go?" she asked.

"It was excellent. And I think God might have said something to me."

"Don't tell me what it was. It's important that I don't know."

"Why?"

"Because I was praying for you, and I think God said something to me for you."

"What is it? What do you think the Lord has said to you?"

"I don't want to tell you."

"What? Why not?"

"I might have got it wrong."

"Well, we can all do that. That's why the Bible says we must weigh prophecies to judge whether they are from the Lord. I can't do that if you won't tell me what you think God has said to you."

"Well, can you come round to my house tomorrow, Arnold? Let me pray about it a bit more first, and if I'm sure, I'll tell you then."

The next day, I went to see Barbara. She knew nothing about the rose vision, but this is the message she believed the Lord had given her for me: "Chile is not for you."

I was stunned. She continued with the rest of the message, "It is not your ambition, but my ambition for you, which is to be fulfilled."

It was a shock, a relief, and an encouragement. A shock because I felt the Lord couldn't have made it any plainer that he had earlier set things up for us to serve him in Chile; a relief because I had found it such a struggle to set up any fund raising visits; and an encouragement because even if we were not to return to Chile, the rose vision suggested that the Lord had something else in mind for us that would be even better.

The following evening, several of us met to pray for further confirmation that the Lord really was speaking to us, since a change of direction would be such a momentous decision, but we didn't get any clear 'yes' or 'no'.

So on Wednesday, I spent several hours in some woods nearby, praying about it. And I had the strongest sense that the Lord was saying that his primary concern was to care for Julian and Emerald, Joseph and Zachary; for Ann, for me, and for both our mothers; and that it was because he cared about all of us that he had brought about this change of direction.

The following day, my mother was told that she had cancer of the throat.

Soon after, my manager at TRADA returned from Chile and strongly advised me to think twice about working at the university in Concepción. Having worked there himself for three weeks, he had discovered that it wasn't a happy place.

Miguel then told me that his church denomination had asked him to take charge of six rural churches in and around the small town of Entre Lagos, which were without a minister. So he would not be allowed to work with me in Concepción after all.

Plainly, the Lord had torn up any plan for me to minister in Concepción or in any other part of Chile, if that really had been his intention. He had put the lid on it and nailed the lid down.

Naturally, I questioned why had he apparently opened up such a wide door for us to return to Chile and had then so firmly shut it. Little did I know that he was about to reveal his unforeseen yet entirely comprehensible purpose in everything that had happened to us—our call to Chile, the people we met there, the fire that brought us back to England, the return visits to Chile resulting in Don Double's encouragement to me to raise money for a new ministry, even Ray Belfield's permission to do that by visiting AoG churches around the country when

I'd had no previous connection with the Assemblies of God—all these things were about to come together like the different colours in a picture. It was as though the Lord had been painting a picture for much of my life and was now asking me, "Can you tell what it is yet?" No, I couldn't. I couldn't see what it was because it all seemed upside down and back to front. But the Lord was about to turn it the right way up!

✿ ✿ ✿ ✿ ✿ ✿ ✿

Of necessity, I wrote to the four people who had promised to support us, in order to explain the situation. I asked them what I should do with the money they had already given us.

[From a letter dated Tuesday April 5th, 1988]

...Have we all been wasting our time? I think the Lord did have a reason for allowing me to start 'Chile for Christ' and to invite you to support us. In 1984, I visited Chile with Don Double. Before we left, a prophecy was made: "Some of your dreams will be fulfilled." On the second night there, I dreamt of being given three large cheques. During the following week, I encountered various situations in which a lack of finance was holding up the work of God's kingdom. I felt that the Lord was saying that I would somehow be able to meet such needs.

A fortnight ago, I received a letter from my friend Miguel Perez. We intended to work together in Concepción, but then his church's governing body asked him to take charge of six rural churches without any minister. Miguel is a faithful and fruitful servant of God, so he complied, but he told me that to pay for their move there, he and Ana had been forced to sell much of their furniture. Their two girls have problems seeing the blackboard at school because they need glasses, which Miguel cannot afford to buy for them. He also said that he would love to have a young man to assist him in his new work and that there are several suitable men, but they have to work to earn a living to provide for their families.

So I feel that if we cannot raise the money to go to Chile ourselves, it might be possible for me to continue to speak at churches about Miguel and Ana Perez's work, and perhaps that of other brothers and sisters in Chile, such as José and Carris Pulgar who are caring for six orphaned girls out of their own inadequate resources. I might even raise enough money to pay for Miguel's assistant and give other financial help to the work of God in that country.

I am sure that it is right for us to share our material wealth with Christians who are very poor, even if there is nothing else we can do. It seems that at present, we are not going to return to Chile, but meanwhile, we can help to build God's kingdom there by supporting Chilean pastors with finance, prayer, and advice as much as we can.

So I want to ask you what you would like me to do with the money you have given us, and what you would like to do from now on. If you would like me to return it to you, I am very willing to do so, since I am no longer going to do what I told you I was going to do. If you would like me to send it to Miguel and Ana, I'd be delighted to do that, and I hope that he'd then have enough to buy glasses for both girls and maybe even for himself. So far as your standing order is concerned, please feel free to cancel it if that is what you want to do. But if you want to continue with it, then of course I shall keep you informed about what is happening and keep you in touch with Miguel and others so that we can be encouraged as we learn about the fruit our gifts are bearing. I shall keep the Chile for Christ fund open. Whatever you decide, please let me know fairly soon because I want to send them whatever remains as quickly as possible.

What was so encouraging, and even amazing, was that all four donors wanted to continue with their standing orders! A friend of mine said the other day that this was confirmation that God was in it, for who would normally want to keep giving money to someone they didn't know?

I started taking steps to set up Chile for Christ as a charitable trust and began asking people I knew if they would like to be trustees. By August, two more people had started to donate on a regular basis, and the monthly income had risen to £40. (This is equivalent to £110 per month in 2025.) I began sending out regular newsletters.

[Chile for Christ, December 1988]

> *Since April, we have sent a gift of £213 to Miguel Pérez and his family for family needs, including the purchase of glasses for his two girls, and dental treatment for his wife, Ana, and we sent another £100 towards the building of a chapel in the small town of Entre Lagos where they are now living. We are sending him £35 per month, most of which is supporting his new assistant.*

> *We have sent a £50 cheque to José and Carris Pulgar, Methodist pastors in Temuco, which they used to help pay for their son's medical course fees. José earns £63 a month, and his son's fees are £30 a month, plus books and materials. We also sent a Christmas parcel to the new church in La Junta, which José and another minister founded last May.*

> *We shall shortly be sending a Christmas cheque to a retired Pentecostal pastor and his wife, who have no pension and are desperately in need.*

> *Please ask us for more information if you would like to support us.*

The new church in La Junta had been established in May that year, by José Pulgar and a minister friend. They had travelled 350 miles south together to a village in the middle of nowhere—La Junta. There they preached for four days, resulting in a new church congregation with 18 adults and 13 children. They later returned in a boat with saws and other tools to help the new Christians build a chapel!

Somehow, without any advertising or unsolicited mailshots, Chile for Christ's income went on growing and growing, and in July 1992, I registered it as a UK charity. The trust deed was drawn up free of charge by our old friend Cedric Brown from Aylsham.

One year later, in August 1993, I left Naphill Evangelical Church to continue my work as an engineer and to direct the charity Chile for Christ. Leaving the church was not my decision. The trustees had decided that after twelve years, a change of minister could be beneficial, and they gave me £10,000 towards the purchase of a house.

Chapter 34. Gifts of Knowledge and Provision

I continued my work for Chile for Christ until 2017, when I finally resigned as Director and handed over the charity's leadership to new trustees. The span of our activities over those 25 years was astonishing.

We assisted victims of earthquakes, volcanic eruptions, floods and forest fires. We provided regular financial support to three pastors and their families, and perhaps £30,000 in total towards the construction of new church buildings; we helped to support three pastors' children through university; set up church libraries of Christian books and Bibles, including Bibles for children; and we provided two consignments of slightly-used protective clothing and helmets with a combined value of around £90,000 when new, to two companies of volunteer firemen.[81]

Among the indigenous Pehuenche people who live high up in the Andes Mountains, we financed the building of eight self-build houses, a furniture workshop for the men, a honey-making project for the women and a horticultural project. We also part-sponsored numerous 'Project Trust' young people from England for their year of voluntary service in Chile.

I haven't reported this or what follows to boast, but to give glory to God, who took hold of my love for the people of Chile—a love that he gave me in the first place—and wove it into a wonderful plan to bless them in ways I would never have anticipated.

---

[81] One of these companies had been involved in extinguishing the fire in our house in Punta Arenas.

Through the ministry of Chile for Christ, we saw many miracles involving words of knowledge and financial gifts…

❧ ❧ ❧ ❧ ❧ ❧ ❧

In the year 2000, Pastors José and Carris Pulgar, well into their sixties, had retired from active ministry. The Methodist Church in Bolivia invited them to go there to provide practical and spiritual support to the appallingly poor people who live high up in the Bolivian Altiplano.

Shortly before their return to Chile in July 2001, I was led to arrange for Chile for Christ to send them a further gift of £150. I didn't know how long they were going to stay there, but as it happened, the money arrived only a day before they were due to leave Bolivia. Unknown to us, they had bills for electricity, telephone calls, food and clothing, which they could not pay because they had run out of money. And they were not allowed to leave Bolivia until they had paid them! The money we sent arrived just in time for them to pay off all their bills, with a little left over, which they gave to a pastor with tuberculosis.

❧ ❧ ❧ ❧ ❧ ❧ ❧

Rodrigo Pérez is the son of Pastor Miguel Pérez. In April 2006, the trustees decided to send Rodrigo a gift of £320 to help pay for his final year's university fees. We had not been asked for this, but somehow, I had an idea that Rodrigo might be in difficulty. I emailed the news to Miguel on Tuesday, May 9th. He replied the same day, saying, "I am sure that God is using the trustees. This morning, I began my prayer time before 4:00 a.m., asking God for a financial miracle for Rodrigo, and that same morning, God's answer arrived, thanks to people who are sensitive to the voice of the Holy Spirit!"

There had been a real possibility that Rodrigo might not have been able to complete his university degree. This answer to their prayers was a real encouragement to the family's faith in God and his care for them, as well as to the trustees.

❧ ❧ ❧ ❧ ❧ ❧ ❧

In 2016, Ronnie Pulgar, José and Carris's son, regularly visited Tierra del Fuego, seeking to establish a church there. He had told us that his travelling expenses were covered; nevertheless, in August, we decided to send him £500 for this purpose. Ronny replied in astonishment, telling us that his travel fund had run out that very month. "Really, our Lord is marvellous," he wrote. "He surprises us every day. There is no doubt that the Holy Spirit put into your minds the thought of helping us so that we can continue our precious ministry on the island of Tierra del Fuego."

❧ ❧ ❧ ❧ ❧ ❧ ❧

In 2007, Miguel Pérez, now the senior pastor of the House of Brotherly Love church in Osorno, invited Pastor Esmenar Pérez and his family to move from Coyhaique to join him in his ministry. Miguel's church in Osorno had been steadily growing, and he needed a second pastor with a gift of teaching to help him disciple the increasing numbers of new Christians there. Coyaique is so isolated from most of Chile by fjords, glaciers and mountains that for Esmenar, his wife Marta, and their two teenage children, it was like being asked to move from Shetland to Manchester or from American Samoa to Los Angeles. Marta had never lived anywhere else, and she was particularly fearful about the idea, especially because it would mean that Esmenar would have to give up his job in a school and rely on church collections for a living. Chile for Christ had promised to help him financially for the first four years while the new congregation grew, but what if it did not grow?

One Friday in October, I sent a short email to Esmenar, asking how he was and what his plans were. I didn't know that Esmenar had promised Miguel a reply that same weekend or that on that same morning, walking to work, Esmenar had prayed, "Lord, if you are going to guide me, please do it quickly." He considered emailing me for advice when he reached the school, but then he felt that this would be an abdication of his own responsibility. Arriving at school, he opened his emails and found my message! He immediately replied, asking what I thought he should do. What a responsibility!

I contacted the other trustees and my church Life Group. The Life Group was a small group of us who met once a week for prayer, Bible study and mutual support, and we had been studying spiritual gifts, including knowledge, wisdom and prophecy. The next day, I sent a reply to Esmenar, including all my Life Group's contributions. Our reply included Bible verses, practical advice, a prophetic word to Marta and some words of knowledge.

Esmenar was overwhelmed! There were things in my email that only he and his wife had talked about, and others that he had not shared even with her. As he translated the words of my email to Marta, Esmenar said it was as if Jesus himself was speaking to them. All their fears evaporated. They knew that the Lord wanted them to go to Osorno the following year, and they began their preparations to move straight away.

Soon afterwards, Miguel wrote to thank us. "An answer from such an immense distance can only be the work of the Holy Spirit," he wrote. "May the Lord be praised!"

Chapter 35. An Angelic Mountain Rescue

One of the many ways God used the ministry of Chile for Christ deserves a chapter of its own.

The South American Mission Society (SAMS) had employed a Scottish missionary named Andy Bowman to help three groups of indigenous Pehuenches build proper houses for themselves. The first group live in an area called Cauñicu in the region of Alto Bío-Bío, about 8000 ft above sea level where the winter snow is deep. Their traditional houses were so inadequate that they sometimes woke up with snow on their bedclothes! After only the first of five new homes had been built under Andy's direction, the project ran out of money. In 2003, it was almost inevitable that he would have to return to Scotland, leaving the remaining Pehuenche families desolate.

I knew nothing of this at the time, but the Lord put it into my head to contact SAMS and ask if they had any projects in Chile that we could help to finance. And, of course, they told me about the self-build housing project. We asked our supporters to pray about it, and in January 2004, someone gave us £5000 specifically for this project. This enabled Andy to remain in Chile that year, complete the second house, and make a start on the third house. But another £8300 was needed to finish all five houses. Since the Pehuenches did the actual building work, the only money required was for materials, and the Chilean government had promised to pay for half the cost of the materials, but only after the houses had been built.

Around Christmas 2004, I began to think about the possibility of organizing a spectacular sponsored walk. Although I was in my 60s, I had the idea of gathering a group of people to attempt to climb all 15 mountain peaks in

221

Snowdonia over 3000 ft high in 24 hours, getting friends to sponsor us if we succeeded. I received so much encouragement, both at church and at TRADA, that I decided to go ahead. Thirty of us, some from my church and some from my workplace, planned to make the attempt in June 2005, in the hope of raising the remaining £8300.

From Chile, Andy wrote: "When the families were together, I told them the fantastic news about the promised donation. It would be difficult to describe the expressions on their faces: a mixture of amazement, joy and disbelief. They were astonished that people in Britain, who they did not know and who lived so far away from them, would be prepared to make such a sacrifice for their families and communities. The families offered prayers of thanks and their prayers for those taking part in the sponsored climb."

Climbing the Welsh 3000s involves walking some 26 miles, the equivalent of a marathon, and climbing a total of 12,000 ft (3660 metres). It is notoriously difficult, especially within 24 hours!

Three people acted as minibus drivers, and the rest of us were divided into five walking teams, ordered according to how fast we thought we'd be able to walk. Being almost 63 years old, I put myself in the slowest team, even though I had been training for five months.

Walking southwards, we set off together for the Carnedd Mountains at 9:30 a.m. one morning in June. The weather was perfect—not always guaranteed in Wales—an answer to prayers that those of us in the church had made at a prayer meeting a week earlier. The Carnedds, the most northerly of the three mountain ranges, include seven of the 3000 ft peaks. Having completed these, we descended into the Ogwen Valley in the late afternoon for a brief rest before climbing the second range, which comprised five mountain peaks. The idea was to complete these five before nightfall, descend into Llanberis, have a few hours' sleep in the youth hostel there, and then set off again at 4:00 a.m. or so to complete the final mountain range, which included Snowdon, the highest mountain, by 9:30 a.m. the following day.

Robert, the youngest member of my team, was annoyingly slow. By the time we set off for Tryfan, two other members of my team of five had gone ahead. I was left with Robert and his friend Lee.

The three of us managed to climb Tryfan, a mountain that stands like a sentinel looking down over Lake Ogwen.

As we made the next ascent to the Glyders, Robert held us back even more. By the time we reached the ridge, he was finding it hard to get his breath. We pressed on at a reduced speed over the chaotic slabs of volcanic rock that litter the mile-long Glyders range. Soon, Robert was complaining of pains around his heart. We were in trouble!

Climbing the remaining mountains in the range was obviously out of the question: Robert was an invalid who could now hardly walk, and only an hour or so of daylight remained. We were nearly 3000 ft above sea level and had no means of communication with the world below. There was no mobile phone reception. There was only one thing we could do: pray.

Lee had said he was an atheist, but I prayed aloud for Robert regardless and asked the Lord to help us. After prayer, Robert said he felt a little better. He was able to walk slowly with us supporting him.

Somehow, we struggled on. Robert was still in pain, and our progress was slow. We carefully made our way down the steep scree at the end of the ridge, and I wondered what we should do. We were approaching a crossroads, or rather a 'cross tracks', by a lake. One way went straight on, heading up to the next mountain on our original route. A path to the right descended through the Devil's Kitchen to the Ogwen Valley. The Welsh name for Devil's Kitchen is Twll Du, meaning 'black hole'. To the left, a less used path went down to the Llanberis Valley, where the youth hostel was. We were still very high up, and it was close to evening. There was no point in continuing to the following two mountains, but should we turn left or right?

All at once, like a mountain goat, a fit-looking young man came bounding down the shale-covered mountainside behind us.

"Are you all right?" he asked, skidding to a halt.

"No," I said. "My friend is complaining of heart trouble, so we are going to try to get him down to Llanberis."

"The Llanberis track is easy to start with," the man said, "but it's very steep at the bottom, and it will be dark by the time you get there, so it would be dangerous. You're safer going this other way. It's steep to start with, but after that, it's easy. You can get through the steep part of the Devil's Kitchen while there's still some light, and if you'll come with me, I'll lead you down. I'm a trainee mountain guide."

Compliant as ever, I took his advice, even though it would take us away from the youth hostel. So far as I recall, the man didn't say anything more. We followed him down to safety in silence. And somehow, once we reached the bottom, he wasn't there. He never allowed me to thank him because he had vanished!

There was a spot near the Ogwen Valley youth hostel where I was able to get a mobile phone signal. I called one of our drivers, and he came and picked us up in the night.

Was our guide human? The first rule of mountain walking is don't walk alone: it's so easy to have a fall, and if you have no one with you to go for help, you could die. So would a genuine trainee mountain guide have been on the mountains alone so late in the day? How was it that he appeared the exact moment we needed his help? How did he disappear without a word? And what kind of trouble might we have found ourselves in if we had turned left and tried to go down the path to the Llanberis valley in the dark, as I had intended?

Of course, there's no proof, but I'm sure our mountain guide was an angel—another amazing miracle of God's protection.

The next day, Robert had fully recovered. After a check-up, it was decided that the pains he had experienced were caused by stretching the muscles around his lungs: they had nothing to do with his heart. If only he had followed the training instructions I had given everyone six months earlier!

In the early hours of that morning, I joined three others to climb the last three mountains. And by running all the way down Snowdon, I completed thirteen of the fifteen 3000 ft peaks in a fraction under 24 hours.[82]

One man on the walk acquired such severe blisters that he had to spend the following three days in a wheelchair! But despite the pain, he had been determined to finish because someone had promised him a lot of money if he completed all 15 peaks. What a hero!

Although not everyone was able to manage all fifteen mountains, between us we raised over £11,000, enough to complete the unfinished houses and fund five more!

When Andy showed pictures of our walk at an Anglican church in Concepción, the congregation was so impressed that they committed themselves to a month-long fund raising campaign of their own and promised to take responsibility for funding the rest of the second housing project in Pitríl.

Andy wrote later, "Some thought the mountains in Wales could not be too high if you were going to scale fifteen of them in 24 hours. So when I showed the photo of the mountain valley with goats on the big screen at the church, their chins hit the floor with surprise and admiration of your sacrifice. Your work has had knock-on effects that have gone a long way further than the money raised, in all sorts of ways."

Hallelujah!

N.B. Altogether, I made five attempts to climb the fifteen peaks in 24 hours. Once I ran out of time, another time I strained a ligament when I was blown over by a fierce gust of

---

[82] I didn't count a mountain as climbed until I was back on the road at its foot.

225

wind, and another time atrocious weather brought the attempt to a premature halt. I finally achieved my goal just after my 70th birthday in 2012! What made it even more satisfying was that, in the meantime, a 16th peak on the walk had been classified as a stand-alone peak more than 3000 ft above sea level, so on my final attempt, I and eight others climbed sixteen peaks! This time, Andy Bowman himself took part. He had completed his house-building work in Chile and had returned to England with a Chilean wife.

Together we raised £13,027 in sponsorship for a horticultural project among the Pehuenches.

Chapter 36. Two Love Gifts from the Lord and Another Deliverance from Death

In the spring of 2014, I had the idea of a cruise down the coast of Chile. My manager at TRADA had once been on such a cruise, and he told me how dramatically beautiful the scenery was.

I looked at a cruise website and found just what I was looking for. It was a 2-week cruise in 2015, beginning in the Chilean port of Valparaiso, continuing all the way down the coast, and then round to the Falkland Islands, Uruguay, and Buenos Aires in Argentina. In the first week, there would be several stops where we could meet old friends whom we had known, worked with, and supported in different parts of Chile.

I showed Ann what I had found. She liked the idea, but was uncertain about whether she would be able to manage it, and in particular, how we would pay for it, for it would cost £2005 each. The price included air fares from England and back, and one night in a hotel, either in Santiago at the beginning of the voyage or in Buenos Aires at the end of it.

After our starting-the-day-in-bed Bible reading on May 19th, I told Ann that we should ask the Lord later in the day whether he wanted us to go on the cruise. That selfsame morning, Ann was reading the previous Sunday's church notice sheet, in which she read Psalm 139:1-10. It included the words, *'If I rise on the wings of the dawn, or if I settle on the far side of the sea, even there your hand will guide me, your right hand will hold me fast.'*

Bursting with excitement, Ann came rushing upstairs to show me what it said. As soon as I read it, I understood what she meant: the Lord was speaking about the plane flight to

Chile (presumably leaving early in the morning), the Pacific Ocean on the far side of the sea where the cruise would begin, and God's guidance and protection once we were there. He was telling us that we could go ahead!

The total cost would be £4010 plus all the expensive extras: new passports, travel insurance, the cruise line's registration fee, shore-side excursions, currency exchange, souvenirs, gifts to our Chilean friends and family back home, and airport taxis. We had just £1450 in our current account.

On Friday August 1st 2014, I received a letter from my former employer's pension provider. It said that ever since I retired from TRADA in 2007, they had been underpaying my pension, so they enclosed a cheque for £4739 to rectify the situation, sufficient to cover the entire cost of our holiday! I didn't keep a record of all the extra expenses, so I can't tell you what the exact total cost was, but I've a pretty good idea!

And that was not all! Ann then pointed out that 2015 would be the year of our 50th wedding anniversary. This was like the icing on the cake—the cruise would be our anniversary celebration! And there was still more icing to come. The 50th wedding anniversary is celebrated as a couple's Golden Wedding, and the name of the ship we would be travelling on was the Golden Princess. And after booking the cruise, I read that 2015 would also mark the 50th anniversary of the cruise line, Princess Cruises. So all around the ship there would be '50' flags, celebrating the 50th anniversary of the cruise line—and our marriage. Hanging on our lounge wall at home is a photo of us standing in front of a sign aboard the ship. The sign displays the words, 'Fifty years at sea'!

I feel sure that the day I booked that cruise, God's angels gathered around his throne and applauded him for the marvellous way in which he had somehow managed to assemble this beautiful gift of love for Ann and me.

What made it even more special was that Brenda Gooding, Chile for Christ's Welsh-speaking Gift Aid Secretary, was able to join us for the cruise with her husband David. On disembarking in Buenos Aires they spent another fortnight visiting the Welsh communities in Southern Argentina.

As you might expect, the cruise itself was amazing in every detail.

One of our favourite parts resulted from an event some years earlier. I had received a phone call from our local Fire and Rescue Service in Buckinghamshire, asking me if Chile for Christ could make use of some partly-used protective clothing for fire fighters, now surplus to their requirements. I eagerly accepted the offer because in Chile all the fire fighters are unpaid volunteers. They are not even provided with protective clothing: if they can afford it, they buy their own.

Although the items we sent were classified as used, they scarcely looked it, and through enquiries with the suppliers, I learned that, if they had been bought as new, they would have cost £55,000 in total! With a lot of hard work, we managed to send everything by air, with the necessary documentation describing it as a gift and not for sale, to the Sixth Company of Fire Fighters in Osorno.

So in 2015, as soon as he knew our cruise ship's arrival date in the port nearest to Osorno, the ever-efficient Miguel contacted the fire brigade and arranged for us to meet them. When David, Brenda, Ann, and I arrived with Miguel at the fire station, we were met by ten firemen lined up side by side in the street, all wearing the correct protective helmets and clothing we had sent them. Twenty firefighters in total had taken the morning off their paid work to thank us in person.

I took the opportunity to share the gospel with them, beginning with an account of how the Lord had miraculously saved our family from the house fire in Punta Arenas in 1981— a story I thought would interest them! "Firemen can save people from a burning building, but only Jesus can save us from the flames of hell," I said. "Just as someone overcome by smoke must trust himself to the arms of a fire fighter, so we must trust ourselves completely to Jesus—we cannot save ourselves." I gave them all Bibles provided by the church in Osorno, which several men asked me to sign.

They had prepared hot empanadas, cakes and other things for our elevenses. We watched three of them slide down the fire station pole, and I had a go as well. Then they gave the four of us, two at a time, a ride in their open-top 1928 museum-piece fire engine. Onlookers clapped us as we drove around the streets clanging the ancient fire engine's bell!

I cannot imagine how God could have set up anything more beautifully personalized than that Golden Wedding anniversary cruise as an earthly reward for our service in his kingdom, just four years before my darling wife went to be with her Saviour in heaven.

✹ ✹ ✹ ✹ ✹ ✹ ✹

Another of God's special love gifts was my house. The way he guided us to buy it was another unusual miracle. Once we had the bank's agreement to a mortgage, Ann and I found three suitable properties we could afford. It was so hard to choose between them! In the end, I asked the Lord to guide me to the best one for us. I opened my precious Bible 'at random' to 1 Timothy 5:8: *'If any one does not provide for his relatives, and especially for his own family, he has disowned the faith and is worse than an unbeliever.'*

I thought about Ann's mother, living alone in a council house in Wolverhampton, with Ann as her only immediate relative. The day might come when she had to live with us. We needed a home with a spare room, preferably downstairs. All three houses had only three bedrooms, which we would need for our family, but none of them had a suitable room downstairs.

A yard or two from the side of one of them—in a district named Totteridge—was an old outhouse. This had once been used to store wood and coal and other things, but it was too small to live in. A flat concrete roof reached across it to the house, and a previous owner had enclosed the space between the house and the outhouse front and back, with doors for access. Knocking out the inner wall of the outhouse would create a larger indoor space, but then the heavy flat roof wouldn't be adequately supported in the middle. The verse in Paul's letter to Timothy was relevant, but it still didn't answer the question. I prayed about it and felt prompted to try again.

This time, my Bible opened at 1 Kings 6:6: '*He made offsets on the wall in order that the supporting beams should not be inserted into the walls of the house.*' Old houses in Britain with oak beams inserted into the walls sometimes need remedial work because dampness in the walls causes the ends of the beams to decay. King Solomon, known as the wisest man who ever lived, overcame this problem 3000 years ago by providing supports for the beams on the inside of the walls.

My thoughts turned to the joist hangers I had tested at TRADA, and to an LVL beam I had been testing more recently. Laminated Veneer Lumber is an extremely strong wood material, and this particular beam was now surplus to requirements at work. If it replaced the inner wall of the outhouse, supported at each end on joist hangers, it would be long enough and strong enough to support the centre of the flat roof, and a substantial new downstairs space could be created at a very low cost.

We bought that house. The asking price was £75,000 but I offered £72,500 on the grounds that we had no chain and had provisional agreement for a mortgage, so there could be a quick sale.

We soon made friends with a young Christian builder who conducted the conversion surprisingly cheaply, installing Celotex thermal insulation on the inside of the walls to make the room habitable.

As it happened, my mother-in-law never wanted to live with us, but the new room became a perfect study for me.

It was only after we moved into our house in Totteridge that we discovered the full extent of the blessing the Lord had provided for us. Although we lived on the edge of a substantial town, there was an entrance to an ancient beech wood only five minutes' walk away. The wood provided four miles of wonderful woodland walks among towering trees, scampering squirrels, banks of bluebells in the spring and beautiful birds in the summer. It was hilly too, which made it an ideal training ground for our charity walking teams.

Ann and I never earned between us more than £30,000 in a year. We didn't start to buy our house until I was 51 years old, so I still can't get my head around the fact that the Lord enabled me to pay off the mortgage in only 14 years, finishing just before I retired in 2007.

❧ ❧ ❧ ❧ ❧ ❧ ❧

In 2013, Ann became seriously ill yet again. It began in May when she saw an internet picture of Jesus as a black silhouette, which frightened her. Condemnatory thoughts followed, worse and worse. She was attended for some weeks by health visitors and was given various medications, which didn't help much. And then a member of my church Life Group received a clear word for her from the Lord:

> *"Your life does not need to be like this. For you to fulfil my purposes there have to be some changes. I have put in place the resources, treatment and health that you will need to get better. Seek this out. Persevere with the treatment. Do not be afraid. My purposes are to prosper you and not to harm you. Do not be afraid to seek proper, accurate diagnosis and therefore proper accurate treatment. Do not be afraid. I have a far happier life for you and Arnold together. It is up to you. Do not be afraid to break new ground and to think differently."*

How we needed that message! For on June 4th, 2013, my wife was admitted again to hospital, unable to talk, eat or drink. After ten days the consultant resorted to ECT, the electroconvulsive therapy that had worked once before. Each session of ECT requires a general anaesthetic and leaves the patient with a headache. But after six such sessions, two a week, there was no progress.

I was asked to attend a meeting with the consultant, two other staff members, and my eldest son and his wife. They all looked extremely serious. The consultant asked me what family support I had, trying gently to show me that Ann was unlikely to recover. But the Lord had told us not to be afraid; that the resources and treatment she would receive would make her better! "Persevere with the treatment," the Lord had said, "I have put in place the treatment that you will need to get better." It was probably most annoying to the three staff members in the meeting that I was unperturbed.

"I don't believe my wife will die," I said. "Please keep trying."

Six sessions of ECT is normally the maximum that any patient would be given, but the consultant complied. And after three more sessions, Ann began to speak again, hesitatingly at first but perfectly rationally. Each day she became a little better. With the help of the National Health Service, the God of all comfort had once again rescued my dear wife from death. But after so long without physical activity she needed physiotherapy, and it wasn't until August 29th that she was well enough to return home and resume a normal life. Afterwards, she did try new things as the Lord had told her to, including the South American cruise!

Over the years, we came to the conclusion that Ann suffered major psychotic depressions due to an excess of cortisol in her brain, a hormone which accumulates in times of stress.

If there could be a re-run of our life, I would give Ann far more understanding and practical support than I did after the birth of our first two children. Choosing between the conflicting demands of work and family can be difficult, but I can see that where necessary, family must come first. No doubt I should also have prayed for her much more than I did.

Most of Ann's bouts of depression—for there were two others that I haven't mentioned—were associated with stress, but that final serious depression in 2013 had no obvious cause.

If we had settled permanently in Chile and Ann had been ill there, would the Chilean health service have been able to help her? Would we have been able to afford 90 days of hospitalisation? I believe the Lord looked ahead and that it was in his wisdom and mercy that he brought us all back to England.

Chapter 37. A Fight to the Death

Six months before my darling wife Ann left this world, she encouraged me to write this book. It was Saint Valentine's Day, 2019, and we had no idea that it would be the last one we would celebrate together. She had been reading Psalm 48:12-14, which says, '*Walk about Zion, go round about her, number her towers, consider well her ramparts, go through her citadels; that you may tell the next generation that this is God, our God, for ever and ever.*'

"You must write it," she urged me. "I want our children to know all the wonderful things that God has done for us. It's treasure that mustn't be lost."

🌿 🌿 🌿 🌿 🌿 🌿 🌿

Our first intimation of trouble occurred three months later, in mid-May.

[Monday, May 20th, 2019]

For two days Ann has been very weak. I had to help her undress last night and put her stockings on this morning. I've had to do the laundry, as well as wash up after breakfast. She isn't eating much, but she doesn't want to see a doctor.

When Ann was in the sixth form at school, she had visited Paris with two school friends. While they were there, she bought a small metal desk calendar on which one could set the month, the date and the day of the month. She had kept this calendar all through her years at university, all through our marriage, and all the way to Chile and back. Yes, it even survived the house fire!

Every morning, she would set the day, the date, and if necessary the month. May 24th was the date that the famous preacher John Wesley put his trust in Jesus for salvation, and it was the last date ever on which Ann reset her calendar. The little round calendar still stands on her dressing table in our bedroom where she left it, telling me every morning that the date remains vendredi le 24 mai.

That day, Ann had no strength at all, and she was complaining of a severe pain in her right side. A 999 call brought some paramedics to the house. They found she had a high temperature and detected that the pain was around her gall bladder. She was taken straight to hospital with a gall bladder infection.

In hospital, a surgeon removed several gallstones and a lot of gunge from Ann, and he inserted a stent. But she remained very unwell.

[Friday, June 21st, 2019. Midsummer's Day]

Yesterday, while I was with Ann in hospital, Mark and Dom (our vicar and curate) *visited her and anointed her with olive oil from Jerusalem. They read two passages from the Bible, which Ann asked for—Isaiah 61 and Psalm 85. Mark said, "I like Psalm 84", and Ann immediately began quoting it from memory. She also recited the whole of the Stir Up collect, which greatly impressed Mark, and she told them how she had been converted through it. Mark and Dom had never heard the expression "Stir up Sunday", and they didn't know the collect! Ann couldn't believe how different they were from vicars she had known when she was younger.*

She told them that she had spoken to a nurse about my book The Date of Christ's Return, and it gave me an opportunity to tell Don and Mark how the Lord had saved us from the fire. Mark was impressed.

They prayed for Ann's healing, and then Mark prayed for her and me together. It was lovely, and I cried a bit.

Various tests and scans were revealing more and more problems with Ann's digestive system, and the wonderful surgeons and staff at Stoke Mandeville hospital did everything they could to save my wife's life. There was a blockage in the tubes around Ann's liver, but she was not strong enough for a full operation, and the two attempts that the surgeons made to clear the blockage from outside were unsuccessful. She developed antibiotic-resistant bacteria known as GRE.

[Sunday, July 7th, 2019]

I resolved this morning not to assume that Ann will die or even to talk about it, but to fight for her recovery using the Word of God. I understand that I don't know what God's will is, and I want that to be done as the number one priority. But at the same time Jesus encouraged us to ask and keep on asking, with the words, "Whatever you ask in prayer, you will receive, if you have faith." I am going to fast[83] for five days this week. I will take her Holy Communion stuff today and read at least some of the Psalms she reads each day.

That afternoon in the hospital, I read through most of the old Methodist Service of Holy Communion. We remembered Jesus's death for us with some blackcurrant juice in an egg cup to represent his blood and a small piece of home-made bread on a saucer to represent his body. I was surprised to read again how much emphasis on sin and forgiveness there was in the service. In Holy Trinity Church, sin was barely mentioned.

---

[83] Fasting means to go without food.

I told Ann we could talk about what might happen in the worst case, or instead we could resolve to fight the illness by faith in the Lord's Word and promises. I asked her if she would join me in fighting, and she agreed. She wanted to join me in my five-day fast, but I told her that I thought she was too weak to do that. I sang 'The battle belongs to the Lord' and read two of the fifteen Psalms that she read every day. Psalm 118 came to my mind, and I shared it with her as something to hold on to. It includes the words, "*I shall not die, but I shall live, and recount the deeds of the Lord,*" the same words that the Lord brought back to my mind four years later, when I was diagnosed with cancer.

I stayed with Ann until the evening, and all that time we were not interrupted at any point. She was speaking so quietly that I sometimes had to lean close to her to hear her words.

Twice she said, "You are doing everything right."

"You are so encouraging, darling," I replied. "You are always encouraging,"

She said, "It has been a very precious time."

We told each other how much we loved each other.

I loved her so very much.

🌿 🌿 🌿 🌿 🌿 🌿 🌿

The following Wednesday, I had a phone call from the hospital. They were hoping that Ann could come home in a week's time! A nurse would manage her injections and someone would help her to wash and dress each morning. They would fit some bars around the toilets, and something to hold on to when she got in and out of bed. They planned to try her out on some stairs later that day to see if she would be able to go upstairs at home, or whether she'd have to sleep downstairs somewhere.

On the Friday I finished my fast and I visited Ann again. I was still alive, and so was she. I repeated the words that God had given me that night years before when the hospital phoned and told me she might not survive until the morning. *'The Lord God is a sun and shield. No good thing does he withhold from him who walks uprightly.'* I repeated many other relevant promises in the Bible, and I commanded the blockage to come out of her.

But then Ann began to cry. She said they kept telling her to sit in a chair, but she was too weak to do so. They told her she must go to the toilet, but she didn't have the strength. All she wanted to do was to lie down. She was giving up hope.

And then I was told that they couldn't arrange home care until July 22nd, by which time she might be too weak to come home.

I could only cry out to God, "Lord, hear our prayers. Lord, answer them in your grace and mercy and power. PLEASE!"

🌿 🌿 🌿 🌿 🌿 🌿 🌿

Back home that evening, I binned a lot of ungodly material I had acquired over the years. I didn't want anything in my life to be an obstacle to answered prayer.

I woke up early the following morning, desperately unhappy because Ann was suffering so much. I couldn't understand why the Lord had made so many promises in the Scriptures that seemed to apply to us, without fulfilling them. *"If you abide in me, and my words abide in you, ask whatever you will, and it shall be done for you,"* Jesus said.[84] It wasn't happening.

I decided to do what Jesus did when he was on the cross and the Devil was tempting him to doubt the promises of his Father to rescue him.[85] I thought back to the moments in my life when God had assured me that

---

[84] John 15:7.
[85] Psalm 42.

he was real—the prayers he answered the fortnight after I committed my life to him; the provision of money for the caravan; the time in Aylsham when he comforted me with Jeremiah's words; Ann's healing the day after her miscarriage and the subsequent birth of Zachary; and all the other instances of his loving provision and grace and power that I have recounted in this book. Yes, I knew God was real, and I trusted him totally, but that still didn't mean I understood him.

I realise now that I had been praying for what I wanted, not, as it turned out, for what God wanted. And perhaps it wasn't even what Ann wanted. Her two great ambitions in life had been to give our four children the best possible start to their education, and to teach English as a foreign language. Both of these ambitions she had fulfilled.

Sometimes, in prayer, we find ourselves in a tug-of-war with God, pulling in opposite directions. What we need to do is to be on the same end of the rope as he is, pulling together against whatever is the real enemy on the other end of the rope.

❧ ❧ ❧ ❧ ❧ ❧ ❧

Wednesday July 17th was our 54th wedding anniversary. Emerald and her husband Jason joined me at Ann's bedside. I gave her a beautiful blue dragonfly brooch, and an anniversary card that said, "I will love you for ever and ever and ever."

She didn't say much.

After Emerald and Jason left to go home, Ann said she didn't think I would be able to look after her in the house. She said, "I want to go home."

I queried, "Do you mean our house or heaven?"

"Heaven," she replied. Then she looked directly at me and said quietly, but firmly, "If God's time for me has come, I am not afraid to go home."

Two days later came a day of decision. Ann had contracted yet another infection, which the doctors believed had given her pneumonia in one lung. Her stomach was bloated and pressing against her diaphragm, making breathing difficult. All they could offer were further antibiotics. She didn't want them.

"Please tell the nurses not to give me any more medicine," she said. "I just want to die in peace. I've done what I can. I'm tired. I just want to go to sleep."

I asked if she had anything to say to me.

"I love you," she said. "And I love the children. But I don't want any more tablets. I just want to be left alone."

[Friday, July 19th, 2019]

A nice doctor came for a serious talk. Ann told him she didn't want any more medical attention. He checked that she understood what she was saying. "Do you know where you are?" "What month is it?" "Who am I?" he asked.

He then agreed not to provide any further antibiotics, and deliberately removed the canula from her wrist. It was a simple procedure, but so, so final! He said they would make her as comfortable as possible, but he couldn't predict how long she would last.

I said to him, "We both believe in the resurrection because Jesus was raised from the dead, and he promised that we too will be raised and will be with him. So we are not frightened, but we are very unhappy."

He said, "I understand."

Ann told him, "You are a very good surgeon."

He said, "Thank you. I know it was your wedding anniversary yesterday. I was only married last year, but if my marriage lasts as long and is as good as yours has been I shall be very happy."

After his visit, Ann looked relieved. She even smiled a little. I love her so much, so very, very much.

Chapter 38. The Finishing Line

Ann came back to the house on Saturday, July 27th. A hospital bed had been installed in our living room and I brought in a single bed so that I could be with her in the night as well as during the day. Two carers came three times a day, and a nurse visited every few days. Ann even had a visit from her GP.[86] She was well cared for, and all without any cost to us, thanks to the Macmillan nursing charity, the local Iain Rennie Hospice at Home and the National Health Service. The day-care hospice served the whole of South Buckinghamshire, but it was located less than ten minutes' walk from our house. God was blessing us, even at the end.

On Monday 29th I decided to read Psalm 85 to Ann. It was one of the psalms on her daily list. Then I saw that Psalm 84 looked appropriate too, and it certainly was. I was grateful to the Holy Spirit for guiding me to them.

I repeated Saint Paul's words, *"I have fought the good fight, I have finished the race"* etc. from his last letter.

I described to Ann how I had finished the Great North Run half marathon, with the Red Arrows flying overhead and the bystanders cheering me on, and how I was so relieved and excited when I saw the finishing line ahead. I told Ann that her finishing line was in sight, and that the angels were cheering her on to finish the race and receive her award for running it so well.

[Sunday, August 4th, 2019]

---

[86] For US readers, GP = General Practitioner = family doctor.

Ann can now barely speak. She sleeps much of the time and is bright yellow! She is on continuous drugs to make her less anxious and relieve pain, and she is very unhappy. I tried to cheer her up. I said, "Our first car died of rust. I was not rusty myself, but the car was, and in the end it had to be scrapped and I bought a new one. In the same way, your spirit is living inside a rusty old body that is wearing out, but your spirit is not rusty and wearing out: it is fine. Soon you are going to get rid of this old car and get a brand new one in heaven. It will be an even better one in your favourite colour, bright yellow like our car. Perhaps that's why you have turned yellow. You are getting ready to match your new car!" I couldn't help laughing. I said, "It's so silly to be laughing when we are both so sad..."

In the midst of suffering, joy. In the depths of despair, hope. At the end of the road, a gateway to a new life to come.

That evening, after a little blancmange and fruit juice, Ann had the strength to whisper, "I want to wake up in heaven."

By the following Tuesday, she had lost the ability to drink. I brought her some more blancmange I had made. When she saw it, she managed to say, "Thank you," and ate a little. In the evening, I wished her goodnight, and she whispered, "Goodnight" to me.

"Thank you" and "Goodnight" were the last words that my beloved wife Ann ever said in this mortal life.

❧ ❧ ❧ ❧ ❧ ❧ ❧

That week I discovered Saint Paul's amazing words in his second letter to the Corinthians, words that were so applicable to Ann.

Though our outer nature is wasting away, our inner nature is being renewed every day. For this slight momentary affliction is preparing for us an eternal weight of glory beyond all comparison, because we look not to the things that are seen but to the things that are unseen; for the things that are seen are transient, but the things that are unseen are eternal. For we know that if the earthly tent we live in is destroyed, we have a building from God, a house not made with hands, eternal, in the heavens.'

2 Corinthians 4:16–5:1

I was reassured that in her spirit Ann was well. In fact, I thought her spirit might even be feeling excited about meeting her Lord and Saviour. I hoped so.

A few days later I read those same words aloud to two of her carers. One of them said, "That's amazing. I felt goose pimples as you were reading that. I almost want to cry. Can I take a photo of it please?"

I held my Bible open while she photographed the verses I'd read and then the rest of the chapter. She took the book from me and turned it over to see what this remarkable book was.

[Saturday, August 10th, 2019]

The carers were a little late this morning and it was good because Ann was awake for once. I spent some time with her reading a Psalm and then the encouraging words from Revelation about the people who have come out of the Great Tribulation and are in heaven. Then I read chapter 21, where God describes the new earth he is going to create for us, when death will be no more and he will wipe away every tear. Although Ann can now say nothing and stares into space, tears came to her eyes. She was crying with me. We were both desperately unhappy, but also comforted at the same time. I said, "The Lord is going to give us both a wonderful reward for all our faithfulness and love and service, I know he is. We are his son and daughter and he loves us both dearly."

That Monday was August 12th, 2019. After breakfast, I moistened Ann's lips with some Appletiser. She groaned when I moved her. I told her that she had completed the work that God had given her. He had done everything that he wanted to do in her and through her, and she had finished the race ahead of me. She would receive an amazing reward.

The carers came at about 12:30, but left her alone. At about 1:00 p.m., Jill from the Iain Rennie hospice came, and we discovered that Ann's body was dead. I thought she had died just before Jill came, because I was praying in the kitchen for the Lord to take her spirit to himself, and then the doorbell rang.

It was a relief that it was over at last.

I sang, 'The strife is o'er, the battle done. Now is the Victor's triumph won... The three sad months have quickly sped, but Ann has risen from the dead...' Being able to sing the mangled words of that famous Easter hymn like that made me so happy.

Around teatime, I went to Tesco's to find something to celebrate my wife's 'graduation'. I bought myself a double chocolate sundae and ate it through my tears.

❧ ❧ ❧ ❧ ❧ ❧ ❧

My wife's funeral service was beautiful. I thanked God for her total faith in the truth of his Word; for her awareness of the powers of darkness and her trust in God's protective armour; for her openness to hearing from God and her courage in sharing what he told her; for her unfailing support in all my decisions, and her encouragement in all my endeavours. Faith is betting your life that there is a God, and that is what Ann had done.

My flower tribute to her took the form of two interlocking hearts made with red roses. I wrote these words on the accompanying card:

> *Darling Ann, our life together was an amazing adventure. Your faith in God guided us through choppy seas into new worlds. You always supported and encouraged me. You were totally the best, and I can't wait to meet you again in the Resurrection! xxxx Arnold*

Chapter 39. Gratitude

Right now, I am not content. I am far from being content. Of course I miss my wife, though I do rejoice in knowing she is already enjoying eternity with Jesus. But more than that, l don't feel finished here yet. Like Moses, the cry of my heart is, *"Let us see your miracles again... the kind you used to do."* [87]

And yet, when I look back over my 83 years of life so far (for I'm not finished yet) I am also profoundly grateful to God for answering so many prayers and for showing me so clearly that he is absolutely real:

> *Lord God, my heavenly Father, I've been through hard times, but you have never left me. You have always been there, giving me courage, comfort and strength. You've given me more than I could ever have deserved. I love you so much.*
>
> *I'm sorry I couldn't do more for you. But somehow, in a way I shall never understand, you love me just for being me. You actually think that you made a good job of me. It's incredible!*
>
> *Lord, if my gratitude is genuine, truly genuine, I want to prove it by willingly carrying out whatever last commission you may have for me before Resurrection Day. Because I love you.*

---

[87] Psalm 90:16 in The Living Bible.

Epilogue. The Resurrection of Jesus

As I have looked back over my life while writing this book, I have come to appreciate more than ever the miracle that took place many years before I was born, without which none of the miracles I have experienced in my life would have happened.

I refer to the greatest miracle of all: Jesus Christ's resurrection from the dead.

It was actually the culmination of several miracles, starting with the fact that Jesus, who is one with God, was born as a human baby. God the creator, in the person of his Son, stepped into the world he had made and became one of us in order to bring us back to himself.

In Nazareth, Jesus grew up into a man like us, yet at the same time, he was able to control the wind and the waves with a word, to heal the sick, to feed 5000 men with a handful of loaves and dried fish, and even to bring the dead back to life.

The Gospels tell us that Jesus then voluntarily submitted to the terrible death of a Roman crucifixion. He did this because his death was the key to unlocking the chains of sin that enslave us and separate us from God and consign us to eternal death. John the Baptist called Jesus *'the Lamb of God, who takes away the sin of the world'*, and the Bible tells us that the blood of Jesus cleanses us from all unrighteousness when we repent of all that's wrong with us, and we put our trust in Jesus to forgive us and give us new life.

On the third day after he died and was buried, Jesus returned to life, to fullness of life. Jesus Christ's resurrection from death by crucifixion has been described by numerous people more qualified than I am (many of them former atheists and sceptics)[88] as the best-attested fact of ancient history.[89]

---

[88] e.g. Frank Morison (his real name was Albert Henry Ross), Josh McDowell, Simon Greenleaf, Lee Strobel, Hugh Ross and C.S. Lewis.

Because he conquered death, we have the assurance we need—that if we make him our king and live for him instead of living for ourselves, then we too shall return to fullness of life and will live with him as our king forever. This will be on a new earth which God is going to create: an earth in which there will be no more wars, no sickness, hunger, suffering or disease and no more death.[90] God is going to restore creation itself to how it was before sin came into the world to spoil it. And all who love Jesus will live with him in the new earthly paradise to come for eternity.[91]

That the God who made us was willing to give his Son to die for our sins in such a terrible way is the greatest miracle of love that we could ever experience. Jesus, in obedience to his Father, voluntarily gave his life for you and me. That has to be the greatest motivation for all of us to give our lives to his service while we remain on this earth. The obedience that God desires is not an obedience that comes out of fear, nor out of self-interest, but out of love for him, who gave his Son to die for us and who gave us everything we have. We love, because he first loved us.

---

[89] You can read an outline of the evidence for Jesus's resurrection from websites such as https://www.equip.org/articles/the-f-e-a-t-that-demonstrates-the-fact-of-resurrection and https://pillar.edu/resurrection-jesus-myth-history. (Both viewed August 2024)

[90] Isaiah 65:17; Micah 4:1-4; Revelation 21:1-8

[91] Matthew 25:41-46 and Revelation 20:12,13 tell us that those who have never had the opportunity to know Jesus during their lifetime will be judged according to how they have lived.

Folk hesitate to buy a book that no one else has read,
But if it has some good reviews, then they might go ahead.

If you have enjoyed reading this book, please consider uploading a few sentences of review to its page on Amazon and/or another online retailer (e.g. Barnes & Noble, Waterstones or Eden) and/or your local bookshop. All you need say is whether you liked it, anything you found particularly interesting or helpful, and who in your opinion should read it. (If you can do this, please do it now while you think about it!)

Other ways you could spread the love:

- Buy two paperback copies for neighbours, friends or family members to help them know that God is real. If everyone who reads the book does this it will go viral! Signed copies are available from https://booksforlife.today with a second copy at half price—two books for the price of four medium lattes at a popular coffee shop, and worth far more!
- Share a picture and your thoughts about the book on Facebook or other social media.
- Tell people about it in your church newsletter, WhatsApp group, blog or community magazine!

I appreciate any help you can give. God bless you! Thank you so much for reading my book.

Rev Arnold V Page BSc, BD, MIWSc, AIMMM.

https://www.arnoldvpage.com

Annexe 1. Knowing God Personally

In the year 2001, a young lady named Kate Middleton enrolled at St Andrews University in Scotland to study Art History. A young man who called himself 'Steve' enrolled in the same course. They shared the same hall of residence, and soon got to know each other. What Kate perhaps didn't know to begin with was that 'Steve' was actually William, the eldest son of the man who would afterwards be crowned King Charles III. William and Kate became friends and in the course of time they married, with the result that Kate became a member of the royal family, and now addresses King Charles as 'Papa'.

In a similar way, it is by making friends with Jesus, the Son of God—and only by making friends with him—that we can join the family of God and know him as our Father in heaven.

God wants all of us to know him, not only as our creator, but as our Father and friend. He introduced himself to us 2000 years ago by coming to live among us in the person of his Son Jesus Christ. Not everyone recognised who Jesus was. As both man and God, Jesus is a unique bridge between God and us. That is why he said, *"No one comes to the Father but by me."* (John 14:6)

All other religious leaders are dead or will be one day: Jesus alone has conquered death, and he is now alive for evermore. He wants to be your friend and guide and helper in this life, as well as saving you from judgment and giving you life for ever in God's kingdom to come. Through faith in Jesus, you can join God's family and call him Father, a father who will accept you and love you unconditionally, whatever your faults or life issues may have been.

Jesus—the way, the truth and the life

Your place in eternity depends inescapably on your relationship with the living Lord Jesus Christ. As Saint Peter told the Jewish rulers back in AD 33, *"There is salvation in no one else, for there is no other name under heaven given among men by which we must be saved."* (Acts 4:12)

The one thing which bars us from living forever in God's wonderful kingdom to come is our sin, just as in the olden days leprosy barred people from human society. Trying to buy a place in God's kingdom by good behaviour would be like a leper offering money to his fellow villagers to let him live among them while he was still a leper. Sin is a kind of inherited virus in our spirits. It manifests itself by our living how we want to live instead of how God wants us to live; by breaking his laws, and by not believing in him and what he has taught us in the Bible. On a wider stage its fruit is war, injustice, family breakdown, greed, envy, lying, cruelty, sexual immorality and marital breakdown, to name only some of its results.

Jesus is the only person who has ever lived without sin, and he is the only one who can deal with our sin and restore us to a right relationship with God the Father. *"Behold, the Lamb of God, who takes away the sin of the world!"* (John 1:29) To do this, Jesus first had to complete a life without sin himself, and then make such a life available to us through his death and resurrection.

Jesus died for the whole world. He died for Christians, Jews, Muslims, Hindus, Buddhists, agnostics, atheists and you! Whether you think you are deserving or undeserving, loveable or unloveable; whatever you have done or not done in the past; however badly people may have treated you and whatever they may have said about you, none of this makes any difference. God wants everyone to be saved and to live in a loving fellowship with himself. (1 Timothy 2:4; 1 John 1:1-3)

With Jesus's help you can begin eternal life here and now, not because you've earned it, nor because you deserve it, but as a gift from the God who loves you more than you can possibly imagine. '*For the wages of sin is death, but the free gift of God is eternal life in Christ Jesus our Lord.*' (Romans 6:23)

To receive eternal life you must put your trust in Jesus to be your Saviour and Lord. That means being genuinely sorry for not living as God meant you to: for all the ways in which you have broken God's laws by what you have done and by what you have not done; by what you have said and by what you have thought; by not loving God with all your heart and soul and mind and strength, and by not loving your neighbour as yourself. It means asking God to forgive you for the sake of Jesus, who gave his life for you on the cross.

Just as Kate Middleton left behind her life as a commoner and committed herself to William to be his companion and helper in all his royal duties for the rest of her life, putting your trust in Jesus means committing yourself to him as the Lord of your life from this moment onwards. It means allowing him to help you to live a new and changed life that brings honour to his Father. This is the only way you can meet Jesus as your Saviour on Resurrection Day, instead of having to meet him as your judge on the Day of Judgment at the end of this age.

Saying "I will" to Jesus

Find somewhere quiet where you can talk aloud to the Lord Jesus. He has been longing for this moment since before you were born. Use your own words, or say the following prayer if it expresses what's in your heart.

Lord Jesus,

I believe you are the Son of God. You know who I am. I realize that because of my sin I am under a death sentence. I am truly sorry for all the wrong things I have done and said and thought. (If there's anything in particular on your conscience mention it.) *Please forgive me. With your help I now want to live the way you want me to and to fulfil the purpose you made me for.*

257

I thank you very, very much that you died on the cross so that I can be forgiven and set free from sin to live for ever in your kingdom.

I now open the door of my life to you. Please come in as my Saviour and Lord, and help me to live for you from this moment onwards.

Thank you, Lord Jesus.

Jesus said, *"All that the Father gives me will come to me; and him who comes to me I will not cast out."* (John 6:37) If you prayed like that and meant it, you can be confident that Jesus has accepted you and restored you to a right relationship with the Father, that all your sins have been forgiven, and that you have the promise of everlasting life.

'*If we confess our sins, he is faithful and just, and will forgive our sins and cleanse us from all unrighteousness.*' (1 John 1:9)

'*For God so loved the world that he gave his only Son, that whoever believes in him should not perish but have eternal life.*' (John 3:16)

First steps

Here are some suggestions for your first steps as a new member of God's family.

(i) Make a permanent note of the date.

It's your new birthday! You'll want to remember this day in the future. '*When someone becomes a Christian, he becomes a brand new person inside. He is not the same anymore. A new life has begun!*' (2 Corinthians 5:17 TLB)

(ii) Tell someone what you have done.

'*For if you tell others with your own mouth that Jesus Christ is your Lord and believe in your own heart that God has raised him from the dead, you will be saved.*' (Romans 10:9 TLB)

(iii) Be baptized.

"Those who believe and are baptized will be saved." (Mark 16:16 TLB)

In the Bible, baptism means being immersed in water by a church leader. It is a way of making public your decision to belong to Jesus, just as a wedding is a way of making public your decision to share your life with someone until death. Baptism doesn't 'save' you. It's how you show Jesus you are willing to obey him, and how he shows you that your sins have been washed away and your new life with him has truly begun.

To be baptized you will have to find a church if you don't already belong to one. Churches can be big or small, formal or informal, dead or alive. A good local church will welcome you into God's family and help you to grow as a child of God. Do an internet search for 'Lively church in Marshmere-under-Water / Little Grumbling / Ambling-by-the-Sea' or wherever you live, to find what's available. If several churches are listed, ask God to guide you, and try visiting them on Sundays until you feel you have found one that could become your spiritual home. Make sure they do proper baptisms!

(iv) Ask the church leaders to pray at your baptism that God will fill you with his Holy Spirit.

Jesus said, *"...if even sinful persons like yourselves give children what they need, don't you realize that your heavenly Father will do at least as much, and give the Holy Spirit to those who ask for him?"* (Luke 11:13 TLB) It doesn't always happen automatically, we have to ask!

The Holy Spirit gives us the power to live as God wants us to. '*...those who follow after the Holy Spirit find themselves doing those things that please God.*' (Romans 8:5 TLB)

(v) Find a mentor

If you already have a Christian friend, ask if he or she would be willing to meet you on a regular basis for a while, to help you to learn how to follow Jesus. If you don't have such a friend, ask if there is someone in the church who would like to help you in this way.

(vi) Talk to your heavenly Father each day.

Find a quiet place to pray and follow the TSP 'teaspoon rule':

Thank God for anything that comes to your mind.

Tell him you are *sorry* for any way you've failed him and ask him to forgive you and to help you to do better.

Ask him *please* to help you, and to help anyone else you know who is in need.

(vii) Read the Bible.

The Bible is like food for your spirit. It will enable you to grow into a strong Christian. If you don't have a Bible of your own you can download one as an app, or else you can buy an electronic or physical copy. There are different kinds of English translation, as well as translations into other languages. Search for 'Bibles for New Believers' to find the translation that would best suit you, or ask someone in the church for advice. If you have never read the Bible, you might find it helpful to start with a very short version of it, written by Philip Law: *The One Hour Bible—From Adam to Apocalypse in sixty minutes*.

Some people prefer listening to reading, and Jesus did once say, "Blessed are those who *hear* the word of God and do it." Whichever way you choose, ask yourself three things as you read or listen: what does this *teach* me about God or myself; is there a *promise* from God that I can believe and claim; is there a *command* here to do something or not to do something? "Blessed are those who hear the word of God *and do it.*"

Further help can be found in *Every Day with Jesus for New Christians*, published by the Crusade for World Revival as a small paperback and as an e-book. Ideally, set aside a time each day when you can read a passage of the Bible, think about it, and perhaps also make some notes on what you learn in a notebook. Ann and I used to read it together every morning in bed before we got up, and then we prayed about what we had read as well as anything else that was on our minds.

Enjoy your new life as a member of God's family. And please introduce yourself to me when we meet in the resurrection!

Annexe 2. The Miracle Song

When a child receives from God a life that's all its own
Or I hear a girl's first word when she has barely grown;
Though a boy's first tottering step may take him by surprise,
At his sudden smile of joy my heart within me cries:

I believe a miracle can happen every day,
I believe a miracle will happen when I pray.
For God's a God of miracles and He only has to say
A word, and things will happen, and a life will change today.

When two people fall in love and laughter fills the air,
When they're facing troubles and they seek God's help in
prayer;
When they put each other first and know how to forgive,
Show by generous hands and hearts how Jesus Christ would
live:

I believe a miracle...

When I'm needing comfort, and I find it in God's word,
See his loving kindness, though with tears my sight is
blurred;
When a loved one leaves this world, and yet my soul can
sing,
Knowing God has more for us than sin and death can bring:

I believe a miracle...

When believers pray as one and faith begins to rise,
Things that were impossible take place before their eyes.
Christ can heal the sick in body, mind and heart and soul,
Nothing is too hard for him whose love can make us whole:

I believe a miracle can happen every day,
I believe that miracles will happen when we pray.
For God delights in miracles and He only has to say
A word, and things will happen, and your life will change today.

You can hear it at https://booksforlife.today/files/miracle-song.mp3. My niece Sarah sings it.

Other Books by Arnold V Page

God, Science and the Bible

God, Science and the Bible tackles head-on hard questions that relate to some of the most debated aspects of creation and the Christian faith. Along with new insights into the argument of design for the existence of God and the viability of the theory of evolution, the author adds his own compelling experiences of God's reality. Anyone who wants to know how the Bible's teaching stands up to questions about the age of the earth, the flood, fossils, carbon dating, ancient trees, etc., will find all the answers here!

Fascinating and engaging, easy to understand, and unique in its approach to proving the existence of God.

Bsmith2 for OnlineBookClub.org.

(This book is also available in Spanish.)

The Date of Christ's Return—Biblical Prophecy in the Final Generation

What does the future hold for Generation Z, the current crop of children and young people? Nothing less than the most exciting event in history! In this controversial and powerfully argued book, science researcher and Bible teacher Arnold V Page contends that Z, the final letter of the alphabet, will also be the final generation that grows to adulthood before Jesus Christ returns to establish justice, peace and righteousness throughout the earth.

It provides a full explanation of Biblical prophecy on the subject, in particular, the book of The Revelation to John.

A fascinating and remarkable portrayal of the world's entire timeline in one cohesive, panoramic form, from a Biblical perspective. Regardless of your religion/value system, I would urge you to read this book.

From a review by Raju Chacko for Reedsy.com
(This book is also available in Spanish.)

Tell me about the Holy Spirit

If the fruit of the Spirit is love, joy, peace, patience, kindness, goodness, faithfulness, gentleness and self-control, where is it? What does it mean to be filled with the Spirit, and how does it happen? Can we demonstrate more effectively the reality, power and love of God to people we meet by living more supernaturally? *Tell me about the Holy Spirit* provides the Bible's answers to such questions. It will show you how to fly!

So many claim to have received the Holy Spirit, yet lack any real evidence. This book will help them to find what they are searching for.

Rev. D. Hathaway. President Eurovision Mission to Europe

The Destiny of the Damned

"How can a God of love deliberately torment unbelievers for ever in hell, especially if they have never heard of Jesus?" That is a question many Christian writers fail to address. In this book, Arnold V Page faces it head on by showing from the pages of Scripture that God will do no such thing, and that while severe punishment does await deliberate unbelievers in God on the Day of Judgement, everlasting torment will not be their fate. Indeed, some who have never had the opportunity to believe in Jesus Christ will have their names written in the Book of Life.

The question of judgement of those that don't ever hear the Gospel message is clearly covered. I'm so pleased to have this pamphlet to share with Christians and non-Christians.

David Lloyd, Amazon reviewer

Unearthly Passion - a Novel for the Z Generation by Vincy Page (pen name)

Unwanted and unloved as a child, Natalie Parsons longs to escape from the moral restraints of her foster family and embark on a life of boozing and floozing at Edinburgh University. Her first-year geophysics course finds her rebelling against the idea that the universe, like her, originated as a meaningless accident. Jettisoning her moral compass, she sinks ever deeper into drink, debt and sexual depravity, until the break-up of a relationship with a lecturer lands her in a life-threatening depression. Rescue comes through a friend who claims to know God, producing a dilemma that only a miracle can solve. Will Natalie ever find the one thing that can make sense of her life—true love?

Brazen T-shirts and outrageous tattoos enliven a humorous and emotional roller coaster of a story that explores the origin of the universe, the truth about God and a reason for living.

"Uplifting through its powerful lessons."

Edith Wairimu, ReadersFavorite.com.

"I only wish that every pastor, parent, teacher, social worker and indeed anyone interested in truth and morality, as I am, would read this excellent book."

Rev G R Hargrove, JP

Twenty-first Century Nutrition and Family Health

This important book explains all that is wrong with current recommendations for healthy eating, and provides clear guidance on a genuinely healthy diet and lifestyle. It is supported by references to over 500 peer-reviewed scientific papers and similar publications. The author's wife ended thirteen years of medication for Type 2 diabetes when the recommended diet corrected her blood sugar level. The author at the age of 70 climbed all 16 peaks in Snowdonia over 3000 feet high in 24 hours.

Available from https://www.booksforlife.today.
I'm very impressed. Brilliant!   Dr David Walton, MBBS

❧ ❧ ❧ ❧ ❧ ❧ ❧

Visit https://www.booksforlife.today for a free copy of *The Way, the Truth and the Life*, 21 very simple Bible studies I wrote for new believers, which were used in Somerset and in Chile.

I am always willing to consider requests to speak on a subject covered by my books. Email brief details and a telephone number to: info@booksforlife.today.